*Current*
**CONTROVERSIES**

# Hate Crimes

# Other books in the Current Controversies series

# Hate Crimes

*Paul Connors, Book Editor*

**GREENHAVEN PRESS**

*An imprint of Thomson Gale, a part of The Thomson Corporation*

Detroit • New York • San Francisco • New Haven, Conn. • Waterville, Maine • London

THOMSON

————— ★ —————™

GALE

Christine Nasso, *Publisher*
Elizabeth Des Chenes, *Managing Editor*

© 2007 Thomson Gale, a part of The Thomson Corporation.

Thomson and Star logo are trademarks and Gale and Greenhaven Press are registered trademarks used herein under license.

*For more information, contact:*
Greenhaven Press
27500 Drake Rd.
Farmington Hills, MI 48331-3535
Or you can visit our Internet site at http://www.gale.com

Cover photograph reproduced by permission of Thomas Wirth/AFP/Getty Images.

LIBRARY OF CONGRESS CATALOGING-IN-PUBLICATION DATA

Hate Crimes / Paul Connors, book editor.
    p. cm. -- (Current controversies)
    Includes bibliographical references and index.
    ISBN-13: 978-0-7377-2208-6 (lib. : alk. paper)
    ISBN-10: 0-7377-2208-8 (lib. : alk. paper)
    ISBN-13: 978-0-7377-2209-3 (pbk. : alk. paper)
    ISBN-10: 0-7377-2209-6 (pbk. : alk. paper)
    1. Hate crimes--Juvenile literature. I. Connors, Paul, 1960–
    HV6773.5.H38 2007
    364.15--dc22
                                                          2006022919

Printed in the United States of America
10 9 8 7 6 5 4 3 2 1

# Contents

## Chapter 1: Are Hate Crimes a Serious Problem?

**Yes: Hate Crimes Are a Serious Problem**

# Chapter 2: Are Hate Crime Laws Necessary?

# Chapter 3: Should Hate Speech Be Restricted?

## Chapter 4: How Can Hate Groups Be Stopped?

# Foreword

By definition, controversies are "discussions of questions in which opposing opinions clash" (Webster's Twentieth Century Dictionary Unabridged). Few would deny that controversies are a pervasive part of the human condition and exist on virtually every level of human enterprise. Controversies transpire between individuals and among groups, within nations and between nations. Controversies supply the grist necessary for progress by providing challenges and challengers to the status quo. They also create atmospheres where strife and warfare can flourish. A world without controversies would be a peaceful world; but it also would be, by and large, static and prosaic.

## The Series' Purpose

The purpose of the Current Controversies series is to explore many of the social, political, and economic controversies dominating the national and international scenes today. Titles selected for inclusion in the series are highly focused and specific. For example, from the larger category of criminal justice, Current Controversies deals with specific topics such as police brutality, gun control, white collar crime, and others. The debates in Current Controversies also are presented in a useful, timeless fashion. Articles and book excerpts included in each title are selected if they contribute valuable, long-range ideas to the overall debate. And wherever possible, current information is enhanced with historical documents and other relevant materials. Thus, while individual titles are current in focus, every effort is made to ensure that they will not become quickly outdated. Books in the Current Controversies series will remain important resources for librarians, teachers, and students for many years.

In addition to keeping the titles focused and specific, great care is taken in the editorial format of each book in the series.

Book introductions and chapter prefaces are offered to provide background material for readers. Chapters are organized around several key questions that are answered with diverse opinions representing all points on the political spectrum. Materials in each chapter include opinions in which authors clearly disagree as well as alternative opinions in which authors may agree on a broader issue but disagree on the possible solutions. In this way, the content of each volume in Current Controversies mirrors the mosaic of opinions encountered in society. Readers will quickly realize that there are many viable answers to these complex issues. By questioning each author's conclusions, students and casual readers can begin to develop the critical thinking skills so important to evaluating opinionated material.

Current Controversies is also ideal for controlled research. Each anthology in the series is composed of primary sources taken from a wide gamut of informational categories including periodicals, newspapers, books, United States and foreign government documents, and the publications of private and public organizations. Readers will find factual support for reports, debates, and research papers covering all areas of important issues. In addition, an annotated table of contents, an index, a book and periodical bibliography, and a list of organizations to contact are included in each book to expedite further research.

Perhaps more than ever before in history, people are confronted with diverse and contradictory information. During the Persian Gulf War, for example, the public was not only treated to minute-to-minute coverage of the war, it was also inundated with critiques of the coverage and countless analyses of the factors motivating U.S. involvement. Being able to sort through the plethora of opinions accompanying today's major issues, and to draw one's own conclusions, can be a complicated and frustrating struggle. It is the editors' hope that Current Controversies will help readers with this struggle.

# Introduction

> *"Since 9/11, special interest extremism . . . has replaced right-wing extremism as the most serious domestic menace to this country."*

The terrorist attacks of September 11, 2001, against the United States has brought greater attention to the existence and ideology of domestic terrorist groups, the vast majority of whom are well-known hate groups. Domestic terrorism is not a new phenomenon, and did not suddenly appear in the late-summer skies of 2001. The Federal Bureau of Investigation (FBI) defines domestic terrorism as "the unlawful use, or threatened use, of violence by a group or individual based and operating entirely within the United States (or its territories) without foreign direction, committed against persons or property to intimidate or coerce a government, the civilian population, or any segment thereof, in furtherance of political or social objectives." Using this definition, past hate groups would include the racist and anti-Catholic Know-Nothing Party of the 1850s; late nineteenth-century anarcho-syndicalists, who viewed labor unions as a potential force for revolutionary social change, replacing capitalism and state and federal governments with a society run by workers; and the 1960s radical leftist Weathermen, whose stated purpose was to violently overthrow the U.S. government. The Council on Foreign Relations reported that between 1980 and 2000, Americans accounted for about three-quarters of the 335 terrorist acts committed in the United States. Most of these acts were committed by right-wing antigovernment hate groups like the "Patriot" movement, Neo-Nazis, Racist Skinheads, the Ku Klux Klan, and Neo-Confederates. Today, most domestic terrorist acts are committed by radical environmentalist, or eco-hate, groups.

Over the past twenty-five years, the FBI has developed broad profiles of left-wing and right-wing domestic hate groups operating in the United States. Left-wing hate groups generally profess a revolutionary socialist doctrine and view themselves as anticapitalists. Their leadership is an equal mix of males and females, and their social makeup consists of single/divorced/separated college-educated agnostics or atheists, ranging between the ages of twenty-five and forty-five. Right-wing hate groups often espouse beliefs in white supremacy or fundamentalist religion, and they embrace reactionary antigovernment sentiments. Their leadership is male dominated and their membership is generally composed of married, high school–educated men and women, ranging between the ages of sixteen and seventy-six.

Since 9/11, special-interest extremism, characterized by the eco-hate groups Animal Liberation Front (ALF) and its sister organization the Earth Liberation Front (ELF) has replaced right-wing extremism as the most serious domestic menace to this country. In fact, in 2001 the FBI named ELF as "one of the most active extremist elements in the United States," and a "terrorist threat." Unlike left-wing and right-wing hate groups, special-interest extremists are difficult to profile because they adhere to strict security measures in both their communications and their operations. In other words, they do not have Internet Web sites as do the Aryan Nation and the New Black Panther Party. Special-interest extremists also differ from traditional right-wing and left-wing hate groups in that the former groups seek to resolve specific issues by using criminal "direct action" against individuals or companies believed to be abusing or exploiting animals or fostering human encroachment on the natural world. Direct action is often criminal activity that destroys property or causes economic loss to a targeted company, ranging from research laboratories to restaurants and fur farmers to forestry services. Eco-hate groups typically resort to arson, bombing, theft, animal releases, and vandalism to achieve their goals. From 1990 to 2004, animal and environmental rights extremists have claimed credit for more than twelve hundred criminal incidents, resulting in tens of millions of dollars in damage and monetary loss.

In recent years eco-hate groups have escalated their violent rhetoric and tactics. John E. Lewis, Deputy Assistant Director of the FBI's Counterterrorism Division, testified before the Senate Committee on Environment and Public Works in 2005 that one extremist recently told the bureau, "If someone is killing, on a regular basis, thousands of animals, and if that person can only be stopped in one way, by the use of violence, then it is certainly a morally justifiable solution." Recent examples of this targeting include the fire bombing of a condominium complex in San Diego, California, in 2003, causing nearly $50 million in property damages; the vandalism and arson of more than 120 SUVs in West Covina, California, in 2003; and the arson of two new houses under construction in Ann Arbor, Michigan, in 2003.

Eco-hate groups receive a substantial amount of funding from well-known and seemingly mainstream organizations like People for the Ethical Treatment of Animals (PETA). The FBI has documented that PETA has raised vast sums of money to support ELF and ALF criminal activities. Further, PETA has used footage from ALF raids for their own legal purposes, and several PETA officials have issued statements favoring the use of property destruction as a means to further their radical goals. In a letter to the United States House of Representatives Subcommittee on Forests and Forest Health, which investigated eco-terrorism in 2002, PETA denied providing financial or any other assistance to any group for terrorist activities. While PETA admitted to engaging in acts of "peaceful civil disobedience" to call attention to animal exploitation by governments and private industry, it denied engaging in terrorism or violence. The animal rights group did admit to funding the legal expenses of ELF activists, but PETA maintains that it had no involvement or connection to any direct action committed by ELF.

From the perspective of ELF, direct action on behalf of environmental protection may be illegal, but such actions are not ecoterrorism. In fact, the group accuses the "federal government in coordination with industry and the sympathetic mass media" of deliberately smearing the activist group with the "label of ecoterrorism." Testifying before the 2002 House Subcommittee on Forests and Forest Health, ELF argued that because the group has been unfairly identified with terrorism the general public has little choice but to view it in a negative light. Contrary to its public portrayal, ELF insists that not one of its direct actions has ever resulted in the injury of a single person. Instead, the environmental activists target the property of those "engaged in massive planetary destruction in order for all of us to survive. This noble pursuit does not constitute terrorism, but rather seeks to abolish it." Although it does not consider itself a terrorist group, ELF "praises individuals that take direct action by any means necessary to stop the destruction of the natural world and threats to all life."

Hate crime in America is a very complex issue. It is directly and indirectly tied to politics, gender, sexual orientation, political correctness, racism, anti-Semitism, ethnic identity, religion, poverty, environmental protection, and several other social conditions. In *Current Controversies: Hate Crimes*, authors from across the ideological spectrum debate hate crimes from their own particular vantage point. Some writers maintain that the problem has reached epidemic proportions while others claim with equal vigor that no such problem exists. Relatedly, some Americans proclaim the need for the expansion of federal and state hate crime laws, while opponents claim that such laws are unnecessary, if not unconstitutional. Advocates contend that hate crime laws are needed to protect minority populations while opponents see such laws as a convenient way to suppress free speech, particularly on today's college campuses and the Internet. One aspect of this fascinating topic that is undeniable is the existence and apparent growth of hate groups in America.

# Are Hate Crimes
# a Serious Problem?

# Chapter Preface

Hate crime in America is widely regarded as a serious problem. Law enforcement lacks statistical evidence of its severity, however, because not enough local law enforcement agencies actively participate in the federal hate crime reporting program. In 1990 the U.S. Congress enacted the Hate Crime Statistics Act, requiring the Department of Justice to collect data from local law enforcement agencies on crimes that "manifest prejudice based on race, religion, sexual orientation or ethnicity." This act was amended in 1994 by the Violent Crime Control and Law Enforcement Act to cover bias on the basis of disabilities, both physical and mental, as a factor in determining whether a crime is a hate crime. Under federal law, the Federal Bureau of Investigation's Uniform Crime Reporting (UCR) system collects the data and reveals the nature and severity of hate crime in America. For example, in 2003 (the most recent year for which these statistics are available), of the 7,489 bias-motivated crimes, 51.4 percent were motivated by racism; 13.7 percent by bias based on ethnicity or national origin; 17.9 by religious intolerance; and 16.6 percent were the result of sexual orientation bias.

The usefulness of the UCR hate crime survey is compromised by the nonparticipation of thousands of local law enforcement agencies. Of the 17,000 such agencies that provide crime reports to the FBI, only 11,909 agencies participated in the survey in 2003, a decline from 12,073 in 2002. Moreover, the majority of these agencies participate only nominally in the survey. In 2003 only 17 percent of the participating agencies reported one or more hate crimes. Without greater local law enforcement contribution, it is difficult to determine the true extent of hate crime in America using statistics. The authors in this chapter base their arguments on many methods of evaluation.

# Hate Crimes Are a Serious Problem in Europe and North America

*Michael McClintock*

*Michael McClintock is director of research for Human Rights First, a leading human rights advocacy organization in the United States that seeks to create a secure and humane world by advancing justice, human dignity, and respect for the rule of law.*

The most pervasive racist violence in Europe and North America is also perhaps the most banal and unorganized: the low-level violence of the broken window, the excrement through the letter box, late night banging on doors, and the pushes, kicks, and blows delivered to the passerby on the sidewalk. The accompanying epithets and threats, the frequent repetition, the threats that are both random and constant, and the likelihood of a blow becoming a beating, a beating becoming a stabbing or a shooting, adds to a pervasive terror.

In many cities, attacks on minorities, immigrants, and asylum seekers have become almost routine. In a Scottish court, Sheriff Michael O'Grady denounced attacks on asylum seekers in Glasgow as "utterly endemic" and concluded they are "committed for sport." He made the comments at a sentencing hearing for six teenagers, who were condemned to eight and a half years in prison for assaulting a group of Iranian men. Similarly, a Glasgow physician who regularly treats victims of hate crimes said asylum seekers were regularly in and out of hospital after attacks and were clearly living in fear: "They come to me with bruises and injuries to their eyes where they have been hit, and sometimes even bigger injuries." A two-year study of hate crimes in the Strathclyde area, which includes

Michael McClintock, *Everyday Fears: A Survey of Violent Hate Crimes in Europe and North America.* New York, NY: Human Rights First, 2005. Reproduced by permission.

Glasgow, concluded in June 2004 that despite a high number of registered hate crimes, only 20 percent of incidents were reported to the police, due to a lack of confidence in local law enforcement by vulnerable minorities. The study, which was commissioned by the Strathclyde police, considered the patterns of attacks, and found that most attacks were not politically charged or orchestrated, but were casual acts of racism against people whose jobs obliged them to meet with the public:

> [A] high proportion of recorded incidents are perpetrated against frontline staff in small businesses, the overwhelming majority of the perpetrators white. The great majority of the people targeted were men from Asian backgrounds. Around three-quarters of those targets worked in small shops and mini-markets, and another sixth worked in takeaways and restaurants. The typical incident was face-to-face, involving verbal abuse, often accompanied by threats or assault. Criminal damage was also common.

---

*This kind of pervasive, low-level (but still potentially lethal) violence is the form of racism that is arguably the most threatening to the largest groups of people.*

---

A similar pattern appears to hold true elsewhere. In Northern Ireland, where long-standing Catholic/Protestant sectarian violence has diminished, immigrants distinguished by their language, the color of their skin, or their manner of dress are increasingly abused verbally, beaten, or firebombed in their homes. On July 22, 2004, the home of a Bangladeshi family was firebombed in Belfast—in what the head of the family said was about the twentieth such attack: "They tried to burn my house, they broke my windows, they smashed my door with a baseball bat—I don't know why they are doing this to me." Belfast police at that time warned of further threats and said 89 racist incidents had been reported there so far in 2004.

This kind of pervasive, low-level (but still potentially lethal) violence is the form of racism that is arguably the most threatening to the largest groups of people, whether in the United Kingdom, Moscow, the Paris suburbs, or in mini-marts or motels in Arkansas or Southern California. There is no single political overseer of or inspiration behind much of this violence, although many voices may join in the chorus of political hatred and incitement that provides its backdrop. There is no direct tie to international events, although the conflict in the Middle East or the fears raised by September 11 may play a part in some of the attacks.

## Ordinary Violence

This emphasis on the ordinary is not to overlook the threat posed by organized hate groups and the extraordinary violence attributed to skinheads and ideological extremists in Europe. The intersection between the ideological extreme and the ordinary is perhaps the most chilling aspect of the current fight against racism. The casual violence of skinheads at a football match or on their own block may be part of something more organized, or organized extremist acts may set a template for the violence of others.

This "ordinary" violence in Europe affects nationals and immigrants without distinction—particularly those of African origin. Attacks on people of sub-Saharan African origin in Europe are both frequent and poorly documented—a particular blind spot in both official statistics on hate crimes and in monitoring and reporting by nongovernmental organizations.

Some of the most horrific incidents involving African students in Europe have been reported in the Russian Federation, particularly since November 2003, when 42 mostly African and Asian students burned to death in a fire in their dormitory at Moscow's Friendship University (the former Patrice Lumumba University). According to students who survived, firefighters made little effort to help and students are convinced the fire was set by arsonists—although the official inquest blamed electrical problems.

African students in Moscow have described living in fear in their dormitories, on the campus, and, particularly, on the way to classes off-campus which require them to travel on public transportation. Students band together, wherever possible traveling on the Moscow metro only in groups, explaining that racist attacks are otherwise almost inevitable. Attacks on African students were so constant that in 2002 a group of 37 ambassadors from African countries addressed a petition to Russian President Vladimir Putin demanding protection. A former president of the Association of African Students told Human Rights First that he and his fellow students warn their newly arrived countrymen about the dangers. "We tell them . . . after about 5 pm, going to clubs and discos—no. We are thinking, 'When can I finish up my studies and get out of here?'"

---

*According to . . . the independent Moscow Bureau for Human Rights, the number of 'skinheads' is estimated at roughly 50,000.*

---

## The Scope of the Problem

The scope of the problem can be seen from a survey conducted by Amnesty International from May 2001 to April 2002, in which a community of Africans living in Moscow were questioned about violent crimes against them. Over the course of the year, the 180 respondents reported 204 attacks, most of them by groups of young adults. When asked about the frequency of hate crimes among refugees in Moscow, a human rights activist told Human Rights First, "A day doesn't go by without a complaint." The international and, indeed, transcontinental dimensions of the Neo-Nazi and related movements are an indicator of the potency of the ideology of racism and exclusion. The emergence of nationalist youth gangs in the Russian Federation, many adopting the regalia of Nazi Germany, may be an extreme example. However, in many Russian cities, racist violence by skinheads is an everyday routine. To some extent this violence is organized. The Organized Crime Unit of the Ministry of Internal Affairs (MVD) now states that there are 453 extremist organizations in the country, of which 147 are "skinheads."

In what has come to be an almost typical, everyday incident in Moscow, a group of armed skinheads attacked an ethnic Tajik family on February 9, 2004, as they entered the courtyard of their apartment house. The assailants stabbed nine-year-old Khursheda Sultonova to death, and severely injured her father and eleven-year-old cousin.

According to Alexander Brod, Director of the independent Moscow Bureau for Human Rights, the number of "skinheads" is estimated at roughly 50,000. An official estimate given by the MVD, by contrast, was about 20,000 "extremists."

## Organized Extremist Groups

The role of organized extremist groups among fans of professional football (soccer) in Europe is also cause for concern. Despite the recognition of the seriousness of the problem, and important actions to combat racism, black, Jewish, and other minority players continue to be subjected to both verbal and physical abuse, and attacks on minorities in and around football grounds continue to be a major law enforcement issue.

British football star David Beckham has joined other sports professionals in the anti-racism battle, telling fans, "We need to kick this stuff out," as part of an ongoing campaign. Racism at football games is addressed by a range of organizations and supported by professional players' associations and unions, team owners, and governments. The European "Football Against Racism [in Europe]" (FARE), a network of organizations from thirteen countries, monitors and reports incidents of racist abuse by spectators, coaches, and players in Europe.

FARE and its national affiliates, like the British Kick It Out, have a hotline for fans to report racist incidents and seek action through football associations to stop racist chanting and violence on the spot.

In June 2004, the football team FC Moscow began the first-ever anti-racism campaign in Russian football, with its team wearing "Moscow Against Racism" t-shirts. Team secretary Youri Belous explained that "For Russia and especially for Moscow racism is a great problem. . . . Fanatics and racists are . . . ready to attack or even kill everybody who doesn't bear resemblance to them. In the last years the number of black players in Russian football clubs increased and most of them suffer from racist abuses. FC Moscow struggles against this social evil."

---

*Racist violence also takes the form of desecration of cemeteries . . . , a means to both dishonor and to intimidate a community and to seek to erase its identity within a multicultural society.*

---

Those who oppose racism in football seem to be striking a chord, as some recent attacks have been reported on anti-racism campaigns. In Sheffield, England, the offices of the organization "Football Unites, Racism Divides" were ransacked in late July 2004, and a store of anti-racist leaflets was set on fire. But despite this setback, Football Unites is now planning to celebrate its tenth anniversary as an anti-racist monitoring and campaigning organization, and continues to recruit football stars to supports its efforts.

## Desecration of Cemeteries

Racist violence also takes the form of desecration of cemeteries and monuments to the dead, a means to both dishonor and to intimidate a community and to seek to erase its identity within a multicultural society. Like the special injury and pain caused by attacks on a place of worship to a community bound together by religion, the desecration of the graves of ancestors and monuments to past atrocities is an injury both communal and personal and a threat both abstract and real.

The desecration of cemeteries and monuments to victims of racism continues to be reported across a wide swath of Europe and North America. In the United Kingdom, some 60 gravestones were reported smashed or toppled at the Jewish cemetery in Birmingham on August 22, 2004. In French military cemeteries, attackers defaced both Muslim and Jewish graves, spraying swastikas, other Nazi symbols, and antisemitic and anti-Muslim slogans on walls and tombs in orgies of equal opportunity racism. In Strasbourg, in France's Alsace region, more than 50 Muslim gravestones were desecrated with swastikas and other neo-Nazi graffiti on June 13, 2004.

The desecration of cemeteries, in particular Jewish cemeteries, and of monuments to victims of the Holocaust was reported in many countries, from Canada to the Russian Federation.

- On July 25, 2004, in Bohumin, Czech Republic, vandals poured paint on a memorial to Holocaust victims just two days after it had been dedicated.

- In June, 2004, vandals toppled or shattered most of an estimated 80 grave markers in the Jewish cemetery of the Czech town of Hranice.

- In Romania, on August 20, 3004, antisemitic graffiti was reportedly sprayed on the wall of the Jewish cemetery in the village of Camaras.

- In the Russian Federation, in April and again on July 15, 2004, vandals attacked the Jewish cemetery in Petrozavodsk, painting swastikas and other antisemitic graffiti on tombstones.

- In Spain, a monument to Catalan Holocaust victims at Barcelona's Montjuic, which was damaged and repaired in early June 2004, was again defaced on June 26, 2004.

- On June 3, 2004, 20 Jewish graves were desecrated in Quebec City, Canada, in the cemetery of Saint-Foy.

---

*Hate crimes and the resulting climate of fear and intimidation can blight all aspects of life for communities under threat while also disrupting the larger society.*

---

As noted, vandals in the United States in May 2004 desecrated the Jasper, Texas, grave of James Byrd Jr., the young African-American who was killed in 1988 when three white men dragged him with a pickup truck. Byrd's murder received international attention and led to Texas hate crimes legislation bearing Byrd's name. The tomb was vandalized with racist epithets and the granite tombstone broken. In March 2004, on the occasion of the passage of the James Byrd Jr. Hate Crimes Act, Byrd's parents told the press that the grave was continually vandalized; members of the Ku Klux Klan were reported to pose for photographs there, and on one occasion left a placard saying "we've been here."

## Hate Crimes Affect Entire Communities

Hate crimes and the resulting climate of fear and intimidation can blight all aspects of life for communities under threat while also disrupting the larger society. Academic studies in the United States have found that hate crimes are often more excessively brutal than similar crimes in which bias is absent, "especially in the case of bias against persons due to their sexual orientation, race, or gender." [According to researchers Karen Umemoto and C. Kimi Mikami] these crimes also are "more likely than other crimes to be committed by multiple perpetrators, a feature contributing to their severity and brutality." Perpetrators' targeting of victims as members of a group makes the violence resonate far beyond the individual—posing a threat to anyone who may be perceived to be a part of the group under threat.

When unknown assailants threw a Molotov cocktail at a Jewish community center that houses a synagogue in Toulon on the night of March 22, 2004, the attack was on the broader Jewish community. Graffiti also aims to intimidate and terrorize, as when on August 14, 2004, in the heart of Paris, swastikas and the words "Death to the Jews!" were spray-painted on a wall near Notre Dame Cathedral.

The drum beat of racist violence is often heard only by those most immediately under threat. The high-profile attacks on places of worship, community centers, schools, and other venues that become the subject of newspaper headlines are the exception. So, too, is the organized violence of skinheads, neo-Nazis, and other extremist political groups, which often deliberately aim to publicize their actions with slogans and public claims of responsibility. But the day-to-day rhythm of racist and bias violence is no less dramatic in kind for the individuals and communities living in fear—and sometimes all the more threatening precisely because the perpetrators are indistinguishable from the ordinary "mainstream" populace.

## Hate Crime Motivations

Bias crimes may be motivated by racist or religious hatred, or by discrimination on the basis of gender, sexual orientation, or disability—or some combination of these factors. A woman may be singled out because she is perceived to be a member of a particular ethnic group and in turn subjected to more intense abuse because she is a woman.

In Europe, hate crimes motivated by gender, sexual orientation, and disability, like other bias crimes, have antecedents in the Holocaust. Campaigns to exterminate Jews and the Roma and Sinti ("Gypsies") and to enslave or murder Slavs were accompanied by a program called "Operation T4," designed to eliminate the disabled, and by the persecution and murder of tens of thousands of Europeans identified as homosexuals.

More recently, reporting on the most serious human rights crimes, from abuses against civilian populations in times of war to "ethnic cleansing" and genocide, has shown how racist violence is often compounded by violence based on gender, with rape and sexual mutilation used as a weapon of war and genocide. This has been reflected in the jurisprudence of the International Tribunals on Rwanda and the Former Yugoslavia and in the statute of the International Criminal Court. These factors are also present in many of the racist attacks on members of minority groups in the streets of Europe and North America, where rape and sexual humiliation may be aspects of hate crimes driven by multiple factors. Women who do not conform to stereotypically feminine behavior, whether due to their sexual orientation or other factors, may be victims of sexual and other violence—because they are women.

## Hate Crimes Are Underreported

Notwithstanding the intersection of racism and other biases, hate crimes legislation and monitoring systems often exclude crimes motivated by sexual orientation, gender, or disability. At the same time, European intergovernmental agencies that have express mandates to fight racism and xenophobia may not address other forms of intolerance—particularly as other agencies have express mandates to address women's rights (based on regional treaty law) and the rights of the disabled. Detailed statistics may exist on violence against women, for example, but often these are not correlated with statistics on other bias crimes. European Union and Council of Europe efforts to combat racism have been distinct from parallel efforts to promote gender equality, in part because a distinct framework of international law and regional mechanisms provides protection for women's rights.

International standards require governments to protect all people within their jurisdictions against discriminatory treatment—and to progressively realize the equal enjoyment of economic, social, and cultural rights. Hate crimes have a special immediacy for those suffering broader systemic discrimination: living in constant fear can add seemingly insuperable obstacles to the exercise of basic human rights by denying whole populations a right to security in their homes, schools, workplaces, and communities.

# Hate Crimes Against Lesbians, Gays, Bisexuals, and Transgendered People Are Escalating

## National Coalition of Anti-Violence Programs

*The National Coalition of Anti-Violence Programs (NCAVP) is a coalition of more than twenty antiviolence organizations that monitor and respond to incidents of bias and domestic violence that affect lesbian, gay, bisexual, and transgendered (LGBT) people.*

The total number of anti-LGBT incidents reported to NCAVP increased 4% [in 2003], from 1,720 incidents in 2003 to 1,792 incidents in 2004. The number of victims tracked by NCAVP member programs also rose 4%, from 2,042 in 2003 to 2,131 in 2004.

In the continuation of a trend that started with the 2003 edition of this report, the number of offenders (which had remained stable or actually declined in previous years) rose by 7% from 2,467 in 2003 to 2,637 in 2004—a rate almost twice as high as either victims or incidents.

The ongoing move away from fewer and fewer perpetrators involved in anti-LGBT incidents is perhaps one of the most distressing findings of this report. It signals a truly retrograde environment in which years of progress resulting in fewer people willing to violently act out anti-LGBT bias has been substantially reversed. With respect to hate-related violence, we are in fact "back to the future."

Seven of [2004]'s reporting locations showed modest to significant increases in reported incidents: Chicago (+16), Colorado (+3%), Columbus (+3), Massachusetts (+30%),

National Coalition of Anti-Violence Programs, *Anti-Lesbian, Gay, Bisexual and Transgender Violence in 2004*, 2005. Reproduced by permission.

31

Michigan (+4%), Minnesota (+71%), and San Francisco (+7%). Areas with decreases in reporting were Cleveland (−71%), New York (−2%) and Pennsylvania (−13%). Houston reported the same number of incidents in both 2003 and 2004. . . .

## Increases in Assaults

Notable trends in the incident data collected for 2004 included significant increases in assaults with weapons (14%), harassment (13%), the number of incidents perpetrated by organized hate groups (273%), the number of LGBT organizations targeted for incidents during the year—67, a 92% increase over 2003 and a not coincidental 50% rise in the number of cases of vandalism and 200% rise in cases of arson.

In looking at the 14% rise in weapons use, there were increases in every category of weapon for which NCAVP collects data.

Large increases were found in the use of vehicles in the commission of incidents (60%), as well as the use of bats, clubs and other blunt objects (21%), and weapons designated as "other" (60%).

While injuries overall declined 2%, that decline was mostly a result of a 15% decrease in minor injuries suffered by victims. At the same time however, the number of victims who sustained serious injuries actually rose 20%. This rise is not surprising given the rise in all forms of weapons use. In other related data, the number of victims requiring some period of in-patient hospitalization rose 23%. Reports of incidents involving rape or sexual assault however, fell 7%.

Unfortunately, the number of murders in the 2004 reporting regions continued to rise, from 18 in 2003 to 20 in 2004 (11%). . . .

## Government Is Not Doing Enough

In the wake of increased public attention to anti-LGBT violence in recent years, most mainstream national leaders now

*Student activist Caitlin Muese, 15, was left unconsious after an alleged gay bashing attack at her Concord, Massachusetts, high school in 2003. The day before the attack she participated in a Day of Silence to promote safety for gay and transgendered students.* © Ed Quin/Corbis.

at least publicly acknowledge—if asked—that such violence has surpassed "acceptable" levels, and most will also now publicly and vociferously condemn egregious incidents of anti-

LGBT violence as wrong. But it is one thing to acknowledge anti-LGBT violence (along with racist, sexist and other forms of abuse) as a pressing national concern, and another to address it with any concerted and consistent effort. The full weight and resources of federal, state and local governments have hardly even begun to be brought to bear on the problem.

And ultimately, the goals and roles of NCAVP and its members are tied to creating an environment in which anti-LGBT violence is in fact unacceptable, if not wholly unexpected. At present, we are a long way from such an environment.

---

*The social and political forces now holding power . . . have now moved to open warfare against all that they hold in contempt, including and especially the LGBT community.*

---

Different incarnations of proposed federal hate-crime legislation that would add sexual orientation and other designations, if not gender identity or gender expression, have floundered for many years in the U.S. Congress. The most recent proposed version—the Local Law Enforcement Enhancement Act (LLEA)—would primarily authorize the Attorney General of the U.S. to investigate and prosecute anti-LGBT crimes as violations of federal civil rights law. However, if passed, LLEA would fall far short of truly addressing LGBT hate, assisting the thousands of annual victims of hate violence or supporting those advocating for victims/survivors in local communities. Additionally, it remains unclear what relevance LLEA would have for some of the most at-risk people within the LGBT community—those of transgender experience.

## Open Warfare Against LGBT People

The current political, economic, and social focus which began with the 'War on Terrorism,' prosecution of the war in Iraq, and the call for federal and state constitutional amendments banning same-sex marriage, continued through the 2004 election season and continued in earnest at the writing of this report, don't bode well either for issues considered by many to either be 'ancillary' to national security let alone those that can be viewed as being supportive of LGBT communities. In fact, it is now clear to most that the social and political forces now holding power are beyond simply opposing issues supportive to LGBT people and have now moved to open warfare against all that they hold in contempt, including and especially the LGBT community. It is then little surprise that LGBT communities are experiencing not only unprecedented attacks politically, but have also been living through an unprecedented and sustained increase in anti-LGBT violence.

The current hyper-patriotic and virulently anti-LGBT environment, continuing economic, military and security concerns, along with strong religious, ethnic and racial dynamics increase the likelihood that the level of hate crimes will rise—particularly against those defined as either being connected to actual and perceived enemies and/or outside the bounds of an increasingly narrow concept of "mainstream" culture. . . .

## Open Political Warfare

In as much as it is important to reference events that occurred during 2004 and their impact on the data analyzed here, it would be near impossible to discuss that data without also referencing events that also took place in the previous year. Though this is often the case in past editions of this report, there can be no doubt that the dynamics that had an extraordinary impact on anti-LGBT violence beginning in the latter half of 2003 were only the beginning of a new environment of hatred towards LGBT people that continued through 2004.

As noted in the previous edition of this report, 2003 was marked by the nation and LGBT communities being embroiled in debates on issues ranging from the U.S. Supreme Court's decision in *Lawrence v. Texas*, that struck down anti-sodomy laws across the country in June 2003, to a pair of decisions by the Massachusetts Supreme Court legalizing same-sex marriage in that state. In addition, the nation experienced the culturally significant popularity of network television selections such as *Queer Eye for the Straight Guy*, *The L Word*, *Boy Meets Boy* and the return of Ellen DeGeneres in her new daytime talk show, *Ellen*. By the end of 2003, the nation had moved from debates about sodomy and examinations of the pop culture to open political warfare. [This was evidenced by] stepped-up efforts by states to prohibit same-sex marriage and President George W. Bush's support for an amendment to the US Constitution banning same-sex marriage that would permanently codify the second-class status of same-gender relationships and LGBT people.

# Hate Crimes Against Muslims Continue to Rise

## Council on American-Islamic Relations

*The Council on American-Islamic Relations (CAIR) is a non-profit grassroots civil rights and advocacy group. CAIR is America's largest Islamic civil rights group, serving the interests of 7 million American Muslims.*

"True patriotism hates injustice in its own land more than anywhere else."

—*Clarence Darrow*

Nearly four years removed from the 9/11 terror attacks, the greatest tragedy to befall our nation in modern history, our country has learned certain lessons that will hopefully lead us to a stronger, safer and more vibrant society for people of all races, faiths and cultures.

Since the 9/11 attacks, the most disturbing legal trend is the growing disparity in how American Muslims are being treated under the law on many different levels.

In order to fully understand the status of civil rights in the post-9/11 era, it is essential that this [viewpoint] offer a documented historical overview of major federal law enforcement initiatives, high-profile national cases and statistical evidence of anti-Muslim discrimination in the United States, particularly those incidents that occurred during the calendar year of 2004.

## Anti-Muslim Discrimination

In 2004, CAIR processed a total of 1,522 incident reports of civil rights cases compared to 1,019 cases reported to CAIR in 2003. This constitutes a 49 percent increase in the reported

Council on American-Islamic Relations, *The Status of Muslim Civil Rights in the United States*, Washington, D.C., 2005. Reproduced by permission.

cases of harassment, violence and discriminatory treatment from 2003 and marks the highest number of Muslim civil rights cases ever reported to CAIR in our eleven year history.

In addition, CAIR received 141 reports of actual and potential violent anti-Muslim hate crimes, a 52 percent increase from the 93 reports received in 2003.

Overall, 10 states alone accounted for almost 79 percent of all reported incidents to CAIR in 2004. These ten states include California (20.17%), New York (10.11%), Arizona (9.26%), Virginia (7.16%), Texas (6.83%), Florida (6.77%), Ohio (5.32%), Maryland (5.26%), New Jersey (4.53%) and Illinois (2.96%). . . .

By far the greatest increase from [2003], in both real and proportional terms, occurred in the area of unreasonable arrests, detentions, searches/seizures and interrogations.

In 2003, complaints concerning law enforcement techniques accounted for only 7 percent of all reported incidents. In 2004, however, these reports rose to *almost 26 percent* of all reported cases to CAIR.

---

*In the months directly following 9/11, Attorney General John Ashcroft . . . rounded up and imprisoned well over 1,200 Muslim and Arab men based solely on pretextual immigration violations.*

---

## Factors Contributing to Increased Discrimination

Although not a scientific study, there are several factors which may have contributed to the increase in total number of reports to CAIR [from 2003 to 2004]. These include, but are not limited to, the following:

1. An ongoing and lingering atmosphere of fear since the September 11 attacks [of] American Muslims, Arabs and South Asians;

2. The growing use of anti-Muslim rhetoric by some local and national opinion leaders;

3. Local Muslim communities, through the opening of new CAIR chapters and regional offices, now have more mechanisms to monitor and report incidents to CAIR at the grassroots level;

4. Following the infamous legacy of the USA PATRIOT Act,[1] other federal legislation and policies which severely infringe on the civil and constitutional rights of all Americans continue to be passed;

5. Increased public awareness about civil liberties and the impact of federal law enforcement initiatives on constitutional and civil rights. . . .

## USA PATRIOT Act

In the months directly following 9/11 [U.S.] Attorney General John Ashcroft, using his powers under section 412 of the now infamous USA PATRIOT Act, rounded up and imprisoned well over 1,200 Muslim and Arab men based solely on pretextual immigration violations. The most disconcerting fact about these mass round-ups was the fact that the Justice Department refused to disclose the detainees' identities, give them access to lawyers or allow them to have contact with their families.

In April 2003, Inspector General Glenn A. Fine reported that at *least* 1,200 men from predominantly Muslim and Arab countries were detained by law enforcement officials nationwide. An August 2002 Human Rights Watch report documents cases of prolonged detention without any charge, denial of access to bond release, interference with detainees' right to legal counsel and unduly harsh conditions of confinement for the over 1,200 detainees. Georgetown University law professor

1. The USA PATRIOT Act was passed after the September 11, 2001, terrorist attacks to expand the authority of U.S. law enforcement to prevent and fight terrorism in the United States and abroad.

David Cole said that "thousands were detained in this blind search for terrorists without any real evidence of terrorism, and ultimately without netting virtually any terrorists of any kind."

---

*The American Muslim community has always categorically condemned acts of terrorism.*

---

In addition to the indiscriminate immigrant dragnet after September 11, several high-profile cases against American Muslims further stigmatized the American Muslim community.

For example, after spending seventy-six days in solitary confinement and being labeled a 'spy' in most media circles; where can Army chaplain and West Point graduate Captain James Yee go to regain his respectability after being falsely accused of treasonous crimes that could have resulted in the death penalty? Where might Oregon attorney Brandon Mayfield reclaim his good name after being falsely linked by the FBI to the Madrid train bombings of March 11, 2004? How does Sami Al-Hussayen resume a normal life with his family after being found not guilty of 'aiding terrorists' while serving as a webmaster and exercising his First Amendment right to free speech?

The American Muslim community has always categorically condemned acts of terrorism and believes that those who break the law should be prosecuted to the fullest extent of the law. However, in order to remain consistent with the constitutional hallmarks of due process and 'equal protection' under the law; it is essential that our law enforcement agencies enforce and apply the law in a consistent manner to all people rather than selectively target people based on their religious or ethnic affiliation.

It is time once again for American society to reclaim its true legal tradition and judge a person on the criminality of their acts; not on the color of his skin or the religion to which she adheres.

# Hate Crimes Against the Homeless Are Increasing

*Michael Stoops*

*Michael Stoops works with the National Coalition for the Homeless, a national network of people who are currently experiencing or who have experienced homelessness, activists and advocates, community-based and faith-based service providers, and others committed to ending homelessness.*

Advocates and homeless shelter workers from around the country have seen an alarming increase in reports of homeless men, women and even children being killed, beaten and harassed. The violent attacks and murders are often directed against people precisely because they are homeless, and thus constitute hate crimes.

On May 28, 2005, Michael Roberts, age 53, was beaten to death with sticks and logs by a group of teenagers who admitted to beating the homeless man just for fun. The autopsy report indicates that Roberts died of blunt-force trauma to the head and body, and suffered a fractured skull, broken ribs, badly injured legs and defensive wounds on his hands. The teens returned several times to make sure the job was done.

In September of 2004, three Milwaukee teens murdered a homeless man at his forest campsite. The teens hit 49-year-old Rex Baum with rocks, a flashlight, a bat and a pipe, then smeared feces on his face. They continued beating Baum until they thought he was dead. One of the boys "hit the victim one last time to see if he would make a sound like in Grand Theft Auto," then cut him twice with a knife to make sure he was dead. They covered his body with plastic and rocks, hoping animals would eat him before the body was discovered.

Michael Stoops, "Alarming Rise in Hate Crimes Against Homeless People in the United States," originally printed in *Street Spirit*, http://www.thestreetspirit.org. Reproduced by permission.

In August 2004, Curtis Gordon Adams, 33, beat and stabbed a disabled homeless man to death, and then licked the blood from his fingers on a Denver sidewalk.

In June 2004, two New York City teens kicked, punched, and finally bludgeoned 51-year-old William Pearson to death in a churchyard. Pearson crawled to the church steps before finally dying of a fractured skull. "His head was a bloody mess," one police officer noted.

---

*Over the six-year period from 1999–2004, the National Coalition for the Homeless documented 156 murders and 386 violent acts against homeless individuals. . . .*

---

Sadly, these gruesome accounts are only a few of many recent assaults and murders which demonstrate the hatred, prejudice and senseless violence faced by many of our country's homeless citizens.

## Hate Crime Statistics

Over the six-year period from 1999–2004, the National Coalition for the Homeless [NCH] documented 156 murders and 386 violent acts against homeless individuals. The violent attacks occurred in 140 cities in 39 states in the United States. The homeless victims ranged in age from a four-month-old infant to a 74-year-old man.

The [2005] NCH [annual] report carefully documents 105 hate crimes and violent acts that occurred in 2004, collected from newspapers and reports across the country. This report shows the geographical extent and the sheer savagery of this wave of hate crimes against the homeless.

Yet many of these violent acts go unpublicized or unreported, making it difficult to assess the true magnitude of the problem. Often, homeless people do not report crimes committed against them because of mental health issues, substance abuse, fear of retaliation, or frustration with the police.

Some cases were also omitted because the victims were found beaten to death, but no suspects could be identified. In addition, this report does not take into account the large number of sexual assaults, especially against homeless women.

## Criminalization of Homelessness

There is a documented relationship between increased police actions that criminalize homelessness and the rising number of hate crimes and violent acts against homeless people.

It appears that violent citizens become emboldened to attack homeless people because their city has responded negatively to the homeless population. These violent attacks occur especially where the city has portrayed homeless people as the cause of unemployment, decreasing property values, vacant storefronts or other problems.

Advocates from around the country have cited the relationship between municipal laws to banish or restrict visibility of homeless people and hate crimes and violence. This overly broad enforcement of the laws passed by city governments specifically targeting homeless people are documented in NCH's *Illegal to Be Homeless: The Criminalization of Homelessness in the U.S.*

This survey of cities and states that violate the civil rights of homeless people concluded that California is the "meanest" state in the nation for poor and homeless people, followed by Florida, Hawaii and Texas. The NCH study also ranked four California cities as among the top 20 "meanest cities" in the nation for violating the human rights of homeless people: Berkeley, San Francisco, Fresno and Los Angeles.

## What Is a Hate Crime?

The term "hate crime" generally conjures up images of cross burnings and lynchings, swastikas on Jewish synagogues, and horrific murders of gays and lesbians. Hate crimes are commonly called bias-motivated crimes, referring to the prejudice of the perpetrator against the victim's real or perceived grouping or circumstance. Most hate crimes are committed not by organized hate groups, but by individual citizens who harbor a strong resentment against a certain group of people.

In 1968, the U.S. Congress defined a hate crime, under federal law, as a crime in which the defendant intentionally selects a victim because of their race, color or national origin.

In recent years, federal bias crime laws have been enacted to provide expanded coverage. The Hate Crimes Statistics Act of 1990 mandates the Justice Department to collect data from law enforcement agencies about "crimes that manifest evidence of prejudice based upon race, religion, sexual orientation, or ethnicity."

The Hate Crimes Sentencing Enhancement Act, enacted in 1994, defines a hate crime as a crime in which the victim is intentionally chosen "because of the actual or perceived race, color, national origin, ethnicity, gender, disability, or sexual orientation of any person." This measure only applies to, among other things, attacks and vandalism that occur in national parks and on federal property.

---

*There is currently no federal criminal prohibition against violent crimes directed at individuals because of their housing status, poverty or homelessness.*

---

The most recent legislation, Local Law Enforcement Hate Crimes Prevention Act of 2005, was introduced in the U.S. House (H.R. 2662) and U.S. Senate (S. 1145) in the 109th Congress. This legislation "authorizes the Attorney General to provide technical, forensic, prosecutorial, or other assistance in the criminal investigation or prosecution of any crime that: (1) constitutes a crime of violence under Federal law or a felony under State or Indian tribal law; and (2) is motivated by prejudice based on the race, color, religion, national origin, gender, sexual orientation, or disability of the victim or is a violation of the hate crimes laws of the State or tribe."

## Federal Law Does Not Protect Homeless People

There is currently no federal criminal prohibition against violent crimes directed at individuals because of their housing status, poverty or homelessness. The NCH aims to include housing status in the Local Law Enforcement Hate Crimes Prevention Act of 2005 (H.R. 2662 and S. 1445) and in future pieces of legislation.

H.R. 2662 and S. 1445 have broad bipartisan support, but through the inclusion of housing status, hate crimes and violent acts toward people experiencing homelessness will be more appropriately handled and prosecuted. Also, if victims know that a system is in place to prosecute such crimes, they are more likely to come forward to report these crimes.

People who are forced to live and sleep on the streets for lack of an appropriate alternative are in an extremely vulnerable situation, and it is unacceptable that hate crime prevention laws do not protect them.

# Homosexual Advocacy Groups Inflate the Number of Antigay Hate Crimes

*Leah Farish*

*Leah Farish is a civil rights attorney with an interest in law enforcement and First Amendment issues. She lives in Tulsa, Oklahoma.*

There is an odd spectacle at some shopping malls and amusement parks. A person is standing on a platform, wearing a helmet that covers his eyes. He wears a vacant look or silly grin as he gropes through the air. He is wearing a virtual reality helmet, playing a virtual reality game. The false information fed to him will cause him to make lots of empty gestures, and maybe even some dangerous ones.

Many well-intentioned people these days are wearing virtual reality helmets, believing false impressions and acting on them. With regard to hate crimes, the virtual reality helmet worn by policymakers consists of inaccurate information from advocacy groups, misleading data from law enforcement, and misguided policy thinking.

## Homosexual Advocacy Groups Overstate Hate Crime Numbers

Advocacy groups consistently report from three to 20 times the amount of hate crime that is reported by law enforcement. The press seems only too happy to report hate crime as growing, often using statistics from private groups, which are not held accountable for their reports.

For example, the National Institute Against Prejudice and Violence has estimated that "the number of college students

Leah Farish, "Hate Crimes: Beyond Virtual Reality," www.frc.org, November 17, 2003. Reproduced by permission of Family Research Council, 801 G Street, NW, Washington, D.C. 20001, 1-800-225-4008.

victimized by ethnoviolence (admittedly a broad term) is in the range of 800,000 to one million students annually." However, FBI statistics on bias incidents on school campuses show 555 in 1992 and 799 in 1996.

Moreover, the Anti-Violence Project claims that in 2001, there were 158 anti-homosexual incidents in Colorado, 205 in Columbus, Ohio, 319 in Los Angeles, 547 in New York City, and 317 in San Francisco. The FBI says that there were 17 in Colorado, 12 in Columbus, 103 in Los Angeles, 38 in New York City and 50 in San Francisco. Let us be clear—even one is too many. But this is such a large discrepancy that policy-makers first should address the discrepancy rather than accepting one or the other source of figures.

Advocacy groups reluctantly admit that their numbers do not match those of law enforcement, but they cite two or three reasons why. First, they claim that law enforcement agencies do not sensitize their officers to cultural diversity or to recognize hate crime. This would certainly explain the discrepancy. According to law professor Frederick Lawrence, "Some localities underreport, sometimes for nefarious reasons like not caring about bias crime or sometimes because their people are undertrained—they don't know what to look for." Says Dianne Hardy-Garcia, executive director of the Lesbian/ Gay Rights Lobby of Texas, "I suspect the statistics on hate crimes are very low because . . . police officers . . . don't exactly know what hate crimes are."

However, every force asked said that their officers do get such training, and many forces either allow openly homosexual officers or have a don't ask/don't tell policy. Many say they meet regularly with advocacy organizations such as homosexual activist groups and the Anti-Defamation League, the latter of which has consistently done significant work in this area. In some places, these groups have input into police training.

Members of the Los Angeles Police Department are required to be certified by the Museum of Tolerance in Los Angeles, run by a private organization called the Simon Wiesenthal Center. Over 36,000 California law enforcement personnel have completed its "Tools for Tolerance for Law Enforcement Program."

---

*It would not appear that police lack training in hate crimes enforcement.*

---

## Police Do Not Lack Training in Hate Crime Detection

Nationwide, several officers said they feel pressure from the media to report more hate crime and have to explain that they can report only what they see. An officer in Santa Barbara, California, says, "You're going to see that disparity, but it's not because the police are not doing their job."

It would not appear that police lack training in hate crimes enforcement. Agencies from all 50 states and representing four-fifths of the U.S population have attended at least one of dozens of conferences on investigating and reporting hate crimes. FBI instructor Wayne Koka has trained well over 1,000 agencies in recognizing and working bias crimes. He postulated in 1994 that lack of training might have caused underreporting at that time, but he noted that two other phenomena might explain the discrepancy—either victims themselves were not reporting, or "human interest groups" were "counting non-criminal incidents."

It is certainly the prerogative of advocacy groups to receive complaints from anyone they want, and to define and tally offenses any way they choose. We affirm their freedom to do this as an important alternative to police being our only information gatherers. A good example of the phenomenon of non-reporting is that of Guatemalan immigrants in Fort Myers, Florida. According to law enforcement officers there, thugs rob Guatemalan immigrants routinely on payday because the victims fear talking to police—about anything. In their native country, they believe, if you talk to the local police, you may well disappear.

## Advocacy Groups Commit a Disservice

But we are being asked to believe that homosexuals are being assaulted by the hundreds and thousands and are cowering in fear of reporting. If this were true, homosexuals would not report minor offenses. The fact is that they usually do report minor offenses, vigilantly. Some hate crimes have even been faked in order to provoke sympathy for political causes. *U.S. News and World Report* reports that one security analyst has documented approximately 100 fraudulent claims of hate crimes.

Often, police receive multiple calls from homosexual neighborhoods on the same incident. If homosexuals are willing to pay the social cost entailed in minor incidents, it is not clear why they would not report major ones.

Hate-inspired incidents must be taken seriously, and we condemn any violence against homosexuals. Perhaps we should take off our virtual reality helmets for a moment and ask: "Do advocacy groups do a service to homosexuals when they encourage them to feel hated and live in fear when there is little basis for such feelings?" Such methods do not help those the organization purports to represent, especially when the group's credibility comes into question. Advocacy groups are not the only ones doing fuzzy thinking and reporting. Former U.S. Attorney General Janet Reno may have worn virtual reality glasses, too. In presenting the latest numbers in January 1998, she said, "These statistics show what we long believed is true: Hate crimes have long gone underreported." In reality, figures of reported crimes by definition don't reveal anything about unreported crimes.

# Reports of Hate Crimes Against Muslims Are Overblown

*David Skinner*

*David Skinner is an assistant managing editor at the* Weekly Standard, *a national magazine. He also edits* Doublethink, *a quarterly journal for young writers.*

The Council on American-Islamic Relations [CAIR] released its annual report "The Status of Muslim Civil Rights in the United States 2004" [in May of that year]. Newspapers (the *Washington Post* in particular) dutifully gave prominent play to CAIR's claim that hate crimes against Muslims increased 70 percent in 2003. Little skepticism, however, was applied to CAIR's shoddy information-gathering or its politicized interpretation of the "data."

According to CAIR, George W. Bush's war rhetoric is to blame for the "increase" in hate crimes. But ours is not a society in which hatred and bias begin at the top and trickle down into criminal acts committed by ordinary citizens. And CAIR's report, along with the way it has been received, proves it. We live in a society of singular, hair-trigger sensitivity to slight, and CAIR is situated at the wacky, exteroceptors end of such interaction. Long before a painful stimulus registers in the reasoning parts of the brain, this hysterical organization screams bloody bias.

Media credulousness is perhaps the strongest evidence that American society is wallowing in gentleness. When someone claims to have been wounded, journalists (the great Victorian Gentleman in [novelist] Tom Wolfe's classic formulation) don't question the witness. Even when the witness clearly has an axe to grind, as CAIR does. Yet common sense begs us to look askance at the evidence gathered by CAIR, which relies entirely on self-reporting.

## Questionable Methodology

CAIR's form for reporting a bias incident is available online. Although the instructions emphasize contacting the police first, and suggest enclosing official supporting documentation, it's not even clear how one would do so. The annual report seldom references such documentation. Which is not surprising, given how CAIR's information-gathering process works: If someone merely emails CAIR with a message to the effect that they were the victim of bias, another "hate crime" is tallied, no matter its seriousness or credibility.

It's almost humorous what tiny offenses pass as worthy of complaint in the CAIR report. That a student at the University of Houston "saw flyers and posters with false and degrading statements about the Qur'an and the prophet Muhammad" is apparently a civil rights matter. That a College Republican at Roger Williams in Rhode Island wrote in a student publication that "a true Muslim is taught to slay infidels" is treated with similar gravity.

Several of the report's examples of anti-Muslim rhetoric (the only prominent ones come from [author and radio show host] Dr. Laura [Schlessinger] and [radio show host] Paul Harvey, the latter of which was followed by an apology) hinge on whether or not Islam promotes killing. But this is even a subject of debate within Islam. Also, that the question should be taken up with some interest by outsiders is, again, neither a civil rights matter nor evidence of hatred or bias. The issue is merely relevant to why al Qaeda and other Islamofascist organizations are at war with the United States. And, to put it tamely, it does not speak well of CAIR (or its purported constituents) that the organization does its level-best to close off such discussions.

None of the press coverage on CAIR's report gives readers a sense of its patchwork quality. Although undermining the USA Patriot Act[1] is the most important item on CAIR's agenda, the report dismisses the legislation in about four paragraphs giving a distorted picture of [controversial Section 215]. Nor do the authors note when their evidence contradicts their thesis of increasing bias and decreasing vigilance against bias: In the same section where its truncated discussion of the Patriot Act appears, the CAIR report discusses two cases of government bias in which the rights of Muslims were loudly and effectively defended.

---

*Quite a number of the sample cases produced by CAIR represent the kind of awkward but individually insignificant difficulties that arise from the meeting of different cultures in a pluralistic society.*

---

In one, the right of a Philadelphia police officer to wear her hijab to work was successfully defended by the Equal Employment Opportunity Commission. In the other case, a judge was forced to apologize and resign for suggesting a Muslim appearing in his court was a terrorist. The report's appendix, too, contains another such story in which a Muslim county employee was allowed to keep his job even though his Friday prayer obligations kept him out of the office all afternoon. The situation was resolved; the employee doesn't need to be in the office and, it seems, doesn't need to make up the hours. "I'm really pleased with [the] result," the employee told a California paper. "They [the county] treated me with a lot of respect."

1. The USA PATRIOT Act was passed after the September 11, 2001, terrorist attacks to increase the authority of U.S. law enforcement to prevent and fight terrorism in the United States and abroad.

## No Proof of Discrimination

Nowhere does the report's lack of rigorousness show more clearly than in the section titled "Sample Cases." "On February 28th," reads the very first item listed as a hate crime, "two unknown males assaulted a Muslim student at Georgia Tech in Atlanta at night. The attackers beat him for no apparent reason and did not attempt to rob him." Which means there is "no apparent reason" to call it a hate crime. Under the same heading are listed several instances of minor vandalism, broken windows, graffiti, a defaced "Iraqi display case" at the University of Wisconsin-Milwaukee Muslim Students Association.

Quite a number of the sample cases produced by CAIR represent the kind of awkward but individually insignificant difficulties that arise from the meeting of different cultures in a pluralistic society. That a Muslim student is asked to remove her hijab for her school identification photo is not proof of discrimination; it's proof that our society hasn't figured out what to do about hijabs in official identification photos. Molehills become mountains in many other cases reported by CAIR, as when Muslim airline passengers singled out for security inspection claim, ipso facto, that they're victims of profiling.

Finally, some of CAIR's complaints don't even pass the laugh test: "A mother called CAIR California to report that on March 14th a school coach barred her daughter from participation in the badminton team because she wears a hijab." Never mind the sourcing problem—it doesn't take great powers of imagination to foresee "hijab" problems cropping up in high school sports programs. The most unintentionally funny—and weirdly sad—incident in the entire report is contained in a *Newsday* article included in the appendix: "A Muslim woman shopping in a Brooklyn toy store was assaulted by a man who slurred Arabs and flung a Mr. Potato Head at her, police said yesterday. The suspect's father later said his son apparently acted out of grief because a friend in Israel had been killed by a suicide bomber in Israel."

Despite itself, the CAIR report does seem to have happened onto some serious instances of bias crime, but they clearly represent only a small portion of what CAIR describes as increasing anti-Muslim activity. So until CAIR can distinguish between real crimes and flying Mr. Potato-heads, it would be best if their work were dismissed as the cheap agit-prop it clearly is.

# Feminists Exaggerate
# the Extent of Violence
# Against Women

*Phyllis Schlafly*

*For over forty years Phyllis Schlafly has been a national leader of the conservative movement. In 1972 she founded the national volunteer pro-family organization Eagle Forum. The* Ladies Home Journal *named her one of the one hundred most important women of the twentieth century.*

If Congress is looking for a way to return to principles of limited government and reduced federal spending, or to help finance the expenses of Hurricanes Katrina and Rita without raising taxes, a good place to start would be to reject the Violence Against Women Act (VAWA) sponsored by Senator Joe Biden (D-DE). It's a political mystery why Republicans continue to put a billion dollars a year of taxpayers' money into the hands of radical feminists who use it to preach their anti-marriage and anti-male ideology, to promote divorce, to corrupt the family court system, and to engage in anti-family political advocacy.

Accountability is supposed to be the watchword of the Bush Administration, but there's been no accountability or oversight for VAWA's ten years of spending many billions of dollars. There is no evidence that VAWA has benefited anyone except the radical feminists on its payroll. The Senate Judiciary Committee held a hearing on VAWA in mid-July [2005], but no critic of VAWA was permitted to speak.

Phyllis Schlafly, "Time to Defund Feminist Pork—the Hate-Men Law," *The Phyllis Schlafly Report*, vol. 39, no. 3, October 2005. Reproduced by permission.

## Violence Against Women Act

VAWA was first passed in 1994 after the feminists floated such bogus statistics as "a woman is beaten every 15 seconds" and "80% of fathers who seek custody of their children fit the profile of a batterer." Remember the Super Bowl Hoax, the ridiculous claim that "the biggest day of the year for violence against women" is Super Bowl Sunday (an assertion conclusively refuted by the scholarly research of Dr. Christina Hoff Sommers)?

VAWA was passed when the Democrats controlled both Houses of Congress and was signed by Bill Clinton in 1994. VAWA is the biggest legislative achievement of NOW Legal Defense and Education Fund (which has since changed its name to Legal Momentum). This tax-exempt organization brags on its website that it "was central to the crafting and passage of VAWA 1994 and [its first reauthorization in] 2000 [and] we are currently hard at work to secure reauthorization and full funding for VAWA 2005."

VAWA assumes fluid definitions of domestic violence that blur the difference between violent action and run-of-the-mill marital tiffs and arguments. Definitions of abuse can even include minor insults and irritations that occur in most marriages or relationships.

A woman seeking help from a VAWA-funded center is not offered any options except to leave her husband, divorce him, accuse him of being a criminal, and have her sons targeted as suspects in future crimes. VAWA ideology rejects joint counseling, reconciliation, and saving marriages.

VAWA refuses to recognize that alcohol and illegal drugs are a cause of domestic violence, a peculiar assumption contrary to all human experience. Numerous studies demonstrate a high correlation between domestic violence and alcohol or drug abuse.

VAWA forces Soviet-style psychological re-education on men and teenage boys. The accused men are not given treatment for real problems, but are assigned to classes where feminists teach shame and guilt because of a vast male conspiracy to subjugate women.

VAWA funds the re-education of judges and law enforcement personnel to teach them feminist stereotypes about male abusers and female victims, how to game the system to empower women, and how to ride roughshod over the constitutional rights of men.

VAWA encourages women to make false allegations and then petition for full child custody and a denial of fathers' rights to see their own children. VAWA promotes the unrestrained use of restraining orders, which family courts issue on the woman's say-so.

VAWA-funded centers engage in political advocacy for feminist legislation such as the "must-arrest" laws even if there is no sign of violence and even if the woman doesn't want the man arrested, and the "no drop" laws which mean the government must prosecute the man even if the woman doesn't want him prosecuted.

It's time to stop VAWA from spending any more taxpayers' money to promote family dissolution and fatherless children. . . .

## Domestic Violence Definition

Most people think of domestic violence as the sad or tragic cases of men beating up women. Assault and battery are obviously crimes that should be prosecuted and punished. But domestic violence doesn't just mean criminal conduct. The feminists have expanded the definition of domestic violence to include an endless variety of perfectly legal actions that are made punishable because of *who* commits them.

VAWA's gender-specific title is pejorative and sex-discriminatory: the Violence Against Women Act. VAWA means violence *by men against women*. VAWA does not include violence by women against women. VAWA's funds are routinely denied to male victims of domestic violence. For example, the Texas VAWA grant application makes its sexist goal specific: "Grant funds may not be used for the following: Services for programs that focus on children and/or men."

---

*Domestic violence has become whatever the woman wants to allege, with or without evidence.*

---

Professor Martin Fiebert of California State University at Long Beach compiled a bibliography of 170 scholarly investigations, 134 empirical studies and 36 analyses which demonstrate that women are almost as physically abusive toward their partners as men. Studies by the leading domestic violence researchers found that half of all couple violence is mutual, and when only one partner is physically abusive, it is as likely to be initiated by the woman as the man.

The term domestic *violence* has morphed into domestic *abuse*, a far broader term. Domestic abuse doesn't have to be violent—it doesn't even have to be physical. The feminists' mantra is, "You don't have to be beaten to be abused." . . .

Domestic violence has become whatever the woman wants to allege, with or without evidence. Examples of claims of domestic abuse include: name-calling, constant criticizing, insulting, belittling the victim, blaming the victim for everything, ignoring or ridiculing the victim's needs, jealousy and possessiveness, insults, put-downs, gestures, facial expressions, looking in a certain way, body postures, and controlling the money. A Justice Department-funded document published by the National Victim Assistance Academy stated a widely accepted definition of "violence" that includes such non-criminal acts as "degradation and humiliation" and "name-calling and constant criticizing." The acts need not be illegal, physical, violent, or threatening.

The domestic violence checklist typically provided by family courts to women seeking divorce and/or sole child custody asks them "if the other parent has ever done or threatened to do any of the following": "blaming all problems on you," "following you," "embarrassing, putting you down," "interrupting your eating or sleeping."

Such actions are not illegal or criminal; no one has a right not to be insulted. But in the weird world of the domestic-violence industry, acts that are not criminal between strangers become crimes between members of a household, and such actions can be punished by depriving a man of his father's rights, putting him under a restraining order, and even jailing him. Family courts mete out punishment based on gender and relationships rather than on acts.

Creating a special category of domestic-violence offenses is very much like legislating against hate crimes. Both create a new level of crimes for which punishment is based on who you are rather than what acts you commit, and the "who" in the view of VAWA and the domestic-violence lobby is always the husband and father.

## VAWA is Anti-Male

When a woman appeals to a VAWA-funded shelter, she is immediately told she must file for divorce and accuse her husband/boy friend of domestic violence so that a restraining order can be issued against him. That would be rational if we were talking about life-or-limb endangerment. But it makes no sense if abuse involves merely run-of-the-mill disagreements for which mediation and reconciliation could be better for all, especially the children. No VAWA programs teach women how to deal with family disputes without resorting to divorce. No VAWA programs promote intact families or better male-female relationships. VAWA has no provision for addressing problems within the context of marriage.

What VAWA does is to promote divorce and provide women with weapons, such as the restraining order and free legal assistance, to get sole custody of their children.

The *Illinois Bar Journal* (June 2005) explained how women use court-issued restraining orders as a tool for the mother to get sole child custody and to bar the father from visitation. In big type, the magazine proclaimed: "Orders of protection are designed to prevent domestic violence, but they can also become part of the gamesmanship of divorce." The "game" is that mothers can assert falsehoods or trivial complaints against the father, and get a restraining order based on the presumption that men are abusers of women.

The Final Report of the Child Custody and Visitation Focus Group of the National Council of Juvenile and Family Court Judges admitted that "usually judges are not required to make a finding of domestic violence in civil protection order cases." In other words, judges saddle fathers with restraining orders on the wife's say-so without investigation as to whether her claim is true or false, and without accountability if it is false. If a hearing is held, the woman merely needs to prove her claim by a "preponderance of the evidence." That means she doesn't have to prove the abuse happened, only that it is more likely than not that it happened.

Elaine Epstein, former president of the Massachusetts Women's Bar Association, admitted in 1993: "Everyone knows that restraining orders and orders to vacate are granted to virtually all who apply. . . . In many [divorce] cases, allegations of abuse are now used for tactical advantage."

The consequences of the issuance of restraining orders are profound: the mother gets a sole-custody order, and the father can be forbidden all contact with his children, excluded from the family residence, and have his assets and future income put under control of the family court. A vast array of legal behavior is suddenly criminalizad with harsh penalties. The restraining order frequently precludes the father from possessing a firearm for any purpose, which means he loses his job if he is in the service or law enforcement, or working for a company with so-called zero tolerance policies.

Nevertheless, one study that evaluated the effectiveness of restraining orders concluded that "they were ineffective in stopping physical violence" and another stated that "having a permanent order did not appear to deter most types of abuse."

## Congress Must Investigate VAWA Abuses

Billions of dollars have gushed forth from VAWA to the states to finance private victim-advocacy organizations, private domestic-violence coalitions, and the indoctrination of judges, prosecutors and police in feminist ideology. This tax-funded network is staffed by radical feminists who teach the presumption of male and father guilt. VAWA gives $75 million annually in grants to encourage arrest and enforcement of protection orders, and $55 million annually to provide free legal assistance to victims (but not to the accused men).

---

*Congress should terminate funding for the Violence Against Women Act—a hate-men law that throws husbands and fathers out of their homes and deprives them of their children.*

---

Rep. Deborah Pryce (R-OH) said during the VAWA debate, "Since 1995, states have passed more than 85% laws to combat domestic violence, sexual assault, and stalking." Congress should investigate how many of these laws were the result of lobbying by VAWA employees using taxpayers' money. VAWA employees are aggressive advocates of the "must arrest" laws (that require the police to arrest one person [you can guess which one] despite the trivial nature of the alleged abuse and despite the woman's plea that she doesn't want the man arrested), and the "no drop" laws (that require prosecution even though reconciliation has taken place). VAWA employees also lobby against the shared-custody laws that respect father's rights. Studies show these "must arrest" and "no drop" laws don't stop domestic violence, but flood the courts with trivial cases (about pushing, hair-pulling, etc.) alongside of real cases of battering that deserve prosecution.

Congress should not be spending taxpayers' money to deal with marital disputes, and courts should not deprive children of their fathers on the feminists' presumption that fathers are dangerous. . . .

An estimated 40% of our nation's children are now living in homes without their own father. Most social problems are caused by kids who grow up in homes without their own fathers: drug abuse, illicit sexual activity, unwed pregnancies, youth suicide, high school dropouts, runaways, and crime. Where have all the fathers gone? Some men are irresponsible slobs, but no evidence exists that nearly half of American children were voluntarily abandoned by their own fathers; there must be other explanations.

Congress should conduct an investigation to find out how much of this fatherlessness is the result of bad government policies and putting taxpayers' money in the hands of a small radical group that is biased against marriage and fathers. Congress should terminate funding for the Violence Against Women Act—a hate-men law that throws husbands and fathers out of their homes and deprives them of their children after a very ordinary squabble masquerading as domestic violence. VAWA is not about stopping domestic violence—it is about empowering radical feminists, using taxpayers' money, to change our culture.

CHAPTER 2

# Are Hate Crime Laws Necessary?

# Chapter Preface

Federal hate crime statutes were first enacted in 1968. They prohibit a limited number of hate crimes committed on the basis of race, color, religion, or national origin. The term "hate crime" gained widespread usage in the media in the late 1980s as a way of interpreting a racial incident in New York City, in which a gang of white teenagers, shouting racial obscenities, killed a black man. At about the same time, the nation also experienced a rash of antihomosexual violence. In response, the U.S. Congress passed the Hate Crime Statistics Act of 1990. This act, however, did not extend federal coverage for violent crimes committed because of bias based on the victim's sexual orientation, gender, or disability. There have been several congressional attempts to stiffen violent hate crime penalties and broaden the federal definition of hate crime. During the 2005–2006 congressional session, Representative F. James Sensenbrenner (R-WI) sponsored legislation (H.R.3132) to broaden the definition to include sexual orientation, gender, and disability. The House of Representatives overwhelmingly passed H.R. 3132, but the bill stalled in the Senate Committee on the Judiciary.

Although the federal government's definition of hate crime does not cover sexual orientation, gender identity, or disability, many state hate crime laws do cover these categories. Currently, forty-six states have passed some form of hate crime law. In most cases, these states have amended earlier legislation that referred only to race, religion, or ethnicity, to include sexual orientation, disability, and gender. Currently, thirty-one states protect the real or perceived sexual orientation of the victim, seven states protect gender identity, twenty-seven states punish hate crimes based on gender, and thirty-one states have hate crime laws protecting the disabled.

# Hate Crimes Must Be Punished More Harshly than Other Crimes

*Frederick M. Lawrence*

*Frederick M. Lawrence is the dean of the George Washington University Law School. He is a civil rights scholar and an expert on hate crime law.*

The last several decades have seen a dramatic increase in the awareness of bias crimes—both by the public generally and by the legal culture in particular—and the need for a legal response. We need look no further than the marked rise in the number of bias crime laws.

These developments, however, can obscure the controversy that often surrounds the debate over the enactment of a bias crime law. For example, during the debate over Arizona's bias crime law, enacted in 1997, one legislator objected on the grounds that "I still don't believe that a crime against one person is any more heinous than the same crime against someone else." Another put the matter more bluntly: "a few Jews" in the legislature were making the issue "emotional and divisive." Acrimony has surrounded the debate over many state laws. Is it really worth it?

This question is not entirely rhetorical. Obviously . . . bias crime laws are justifiable and constitutional. But to a large extent, I have assumed the need to punish hate as my starting point. The implicit premise of the task has been to provide justifications for the punishment of racially motivated violence in criminal law doctrine, and to square this punishment with free expression doctrine. . . .

# Are Hate Crime Laws Necessary?

It is wise to step back from this assumption, to ask not merely whether it is justified to punish hate, but whether it is *necessary* to punish hate. A state may do so—but should it? The question is clearer if not conceived as a choice between punishing bias crimes and not doing so. Were the choice truly this stark, the answer would be obvious and compelling. One of the arguments advanced for including sexual orientation in bias crime statutes, for example, is that assaults against gays and lesbians are notoriously under-investigated by the police and under-prosecuted by local district attorneys. (A similar argument is often made concerning laws aimed at domestic violence.) The obvious and compelling response to this situation is that "gay bashing," like domestic violence, should be properly treated by the criminal justice system. The argument based on under-enforcement, however, does not support the conclusion that violence motivated by the victim's sexual orientation should be a bias crime, because it is based on a false choice or, better put, an incomplete choice. The choice between punishing gay bashing as a bias crime or not punishing it at all omits the option of properly handling these crimes as parallel assaults, without regard to the bias motivation. If these cases were investigated as carefully and prosecuted as vigorously as any other assault, then our concerns would be satisfied without the need to include sexual orientation in a bias crime law. One could argue that including sexual orientation is the best way, or perhaps the only way, to improve the manner in which the criminal justice system responds to these crimes. If true, it represents a strong, fairly obvious, justification. But, to be tested properly, the "Is it really worth it?" question must assume that the criminal justice system otherwise works or could be made to work. Is it really worth the acrimony that often accompanies the debates over bias crime laws, to prosecute these crimes *as* bias crimes?...

# Hate Crime Laws Express Social Condemnation of Bigotry

What happens when proposed bias crime legislation becomes law? This act of law-making constitutes a societal condemnation of racism, religious intolerance, and other forms of bigotry that are covered by that law. Moreover, every act of condemnation is dialectically twinning with an act of expression of values—in [French sociologist Émile] Durkheim's terms, social cohesion. Punishment not only signals the border between that which is permitted and that which is proscribed, but also denounces that which is rejected and announces that which is embraced. Because racial harmony and equality are among the highest values held in our society, crimes that violate these values should be punished and must be punished specifically as bias crimes. Similarly, bias crimes must be punished more harshly than crimes that, although otherwise similar, do not violate these values. Moreover, racial harmony and equality are not values that exist only, or even primarily, in an abstract sense. The particular biases that are implicated by bias crimes are connected with a real, extended history of grave injustices to the victim groups, resulting in enormous suffering and loss. In many ways these injustices, and their legacies, persist.

# There Is No Neutral Position on Hate Crimes

What happens if bias crimes are not expressly punished in a criminal justice system, or, if expressly punished, are not punished more harshly than parallel crimes? Here, too, a message is expressed by the legislation, a message that racial harmony and equality are not among the highest values held by the community. Put differently, it is impossible for the punishment choices made by the society *not* to express societal values. There is no neutral position, no middle ground. The only question is the content of that expresssion and the resulting statement of those values.

Two cases, one of which involves the debate over a bias crime law, illustrate the point. Consider first the case of the creation of a legal holiday to commemorate the birth of Dr. Martin Luther King, Jr. Once the idea of such a holiday gained widespread attention, the federal government and most states created Martin Luther King Day within a relatively short period of time. It was impossible, however, for a state to take "no position" on the holiday. Several states, including South Carolina, Arizona, New Hampshire, North Carolina, and Texas, did not immediately adopt the holiday. These states were perceived generally as rejecting the holiday. More significantly, they were perceived as rejecting the values associated with Dr. King, which were to be commemorated by the holiday marking his birthday. Civil rights groups brought pressure against these states with economic boycotts and the like. Once ignited, the debate over Martin Luther King Day thus became one in which there was no neutral position. The lack of legislation was a rejection of the holiday and the values with which it was associated.

---

*Conduct that is more offensive to society should receive relatively greater punishment than that which is less offensive.*

---

The second case concerns the debate in 1997 over a bias crime law in Georgia, the site of one of the most acrimonious legislative battles over such legislation. The tension surrounding the debate was heightened by the bombing that year of a lesbian nightclub in Atlanta. Ultimately, the legislation failed to reach the floor of the Georgia legislature for a vote. As with Martin Luther King Day, there was no middle position for Georgia to adopt. Either a bias crime law would be established, with the attending expression of certain values, or it would not, with a rejection of these values and an expression of other, antithetical values. The values expressed by the rejection of the law are aptly caught by the unusually blunt view of one Georgia legislator: "What's the big deal about a few swastikas on a synagogue?" Others derided the legislation as the "Queer Bill."

## Hate Crimes Hurt Society

Thus far we have considered the enactment of a bias crime law to be a simple binary choice: a legislature enacts a bias crime law or it does not. To do so denounces racial hatred, and to fail to do so gives comfort to the racist. We can make a similar observation in the more subtle context of establishing grades of crimes and levels of criminal punishment. . . . Conduct that is more offensive to society should receive relatively greater punishment than that which is less offensive. We would be shocked if a legislature punished shoplifting equally with aggravated assault. We might disagree as to whether one was punished excessively or the other insufficiently, but we would agree that these crimes ought not to be treated identically. Society's most cherished values will be reflected in the criminal law by applying the harshest penalties to those crimes that violate these values. There will certainly be lesser penalties for those crimes that in some respects are similar but do not violate these values. The hierarchy of societal values involved in criminal conduct will thus be reflected by the lesser crime's status as a lesser offense included within the more serious crime.

## Hate Crimes Demand Enhanced Punishment

The enshrinement of racial harmony and equality among our highest values not only calls for independent punishment of racially motivated violence as a bias crime and not merely as a parallel crime; it also calls for enhanced punishment of bias crimes over parallel crimes. If bias crimes are not punished more harshly than parallel crimes, the implicit message expressed by the criminal justice system is that racial harmony and equality are not among the highest values in our society. If a racially motivated assault is punished identically to a parallel assault, the racial motivation of the bias crime is rendered largely irrelevant and thus not part of that which is condemned. The individual victim, the target community, and indeed the society at large thus suffer the twin insults akin to those suffered by the narrator of Ralph Ellison's *Invisible Man*. Not only has the crime itself occurred, but the underlying hatred of the crime is invisible to the eyes of the legal system. The punishment of bias crimes as argued for in this [viewpoint], therefore, is necessary for the full expression of commitment to American values of equality of treatment and opportunity. . . .

---

*The unique harm caused by bias crimes not only justifies their enhanced punishment, but compels it.*

---

## Hate Crime Laws Are Only Part of the Answer to Racism

It has been more than forty years since [psychologist] Gordon Allport, in *The Nature of Prejudice*, asked whether America would continue to make progress toward tolerance and stand as a "staunch defender of the right to be the same or different," or whether "a fatal retrogression will set in." Laws that identify racially motivated violence for enhanced punishment are only one means of answering Allport's call, but they do constitute a critical element in the defense of the "right to be the same or different." Racially motivated violence is different from other forms of violence. When bias crimes are compared with parallel crimes, something more may be said: bias crimes are worse. They are worse in a manner that is relevant to setting levels of criminal punishment. The unique harm caused by bias crimes not only justifies their enhanced punishment, but compels it.

Bias crimes ought to single out criminal conduct that is motivated by racial animus. Discriminatory selection of a victim will ordinarily be part of racial animus. Indeed, we would expect that the proof of animus in the prosecution of a bias crime will begin with evidence relating to victim selection. Elements of proof, however, must not be confused with the gravamen of the crime. The gravamen of a bias crime is the animus of the accused.

The punishment of hate will not end bigotry in society. That great goal requires the work not only of the criminal justice system but also of all aspects of civil life, public and private. Criminal punishment is indeed a crude tool and a blunt instrument. [The French philosopher] Montesquieu foresaw that "as freedom advances, the severity of the penal law decreases." We are not yet, however, in the world that Montesquieu envisioned. We inhabit a time and a culture that continue to suffer from bias in general and bias crimes in particular. But our inability to solve the entire problem should not dissuade us from dealing with parts of the problem. If we are to be "staunch defender[s] of the right to be the same or different," we cannot desist from this task.

# Hate Crime Laws Are Needed to Protect Children

*Jan Ireland*

*Jan Ireland is a freelance writer whose work is widely posted on the Internet.*

Yet another mother is on trial for killing her children. Again in Texas a woman who gave birth to and nurtured her children for a time has become their killer.

Again we hear the protestations of wonderful mother, devoted wife, and no mother in her right mind could do such a thing. People call for helping the "victim" mother. Such calls are simply giving the killer an out.

Attention should be on the real victims, the children, who have been the focus of hate.

Hate crime designation is suggested for skin color, homosexuality, or other "approved" attributes, but never similarly for these littlest victims.

Murder is murder. "Special" reasons are an attempt at victim status, to filch money or force society to accept an agenda. But surely if there were "hate" crimes, the murdering of innocent children by the mother who bore them would qualify. Society's worth is reflected in how it treats its tiniest members.

## Murder in Texas

Deanna Laney [a housewife in New Chapel Hill, Texas], called police a little after midnight on Mother's Day weekend [in 2003]. In a calm, flat and markedly cooperative voice she told police that she had just killed her three children.

The 911 tape is eerie in its details. Perhaps the youngest wasn't quite dead, she said, and perhaps maybe she wasn't ac-

Jan Ireland, "Mother Murdered Children Never Considered Hate Crimes," renewameri ca.us, March 31, 2004. Reproduced by permission.

tually supposed to kill him. When asked who told her to do it, she responded "God" did.

And that is where she seals her fate. She began with 14 month old Aaron, the baby. Parents are always attuned to a baby's cry, and babies always cry if something disturbs them in the night. Aaron had to be first to keep her husband from waking up. Perhaps he was practice also, before she attacked his older and stronger brothers.

In fact Aaron did wail as she beat his head with a heavy stone. What baby wouldn't? But though it woke her husband, Dee persuaded him nothing was amiss. He returned unknowing to sleep.

She returned to attempting to end their youngest child's life.

Chronologically, she next woke Luke and led him outside, then asked him to put his head (reminiscent of Abraham sacrificing Isaac perhaps) on a large stone. Eight year old Joshua struggled after the first blow, and she had to use her body to pin him down, in a repeat scene a few minutes later.

## Similar Incidents Happened Before

We've seen these circumstances before. Family very religious; living rurally; mother at home with and schooling children every day; regular church attendance. The perfect family. This never expected.

Several psychiatrists—for the defense, for the prosecution, for the judge—have all concluded that Deanna Laney is mentally ill. But Texas law demands more.

Though her plea to capital murder charges is not guilty by reason of insanity, the prosecutor plans to show that she knew right from wrong as she committed the crimes, despite any mental illness.

And he has a strong case. You can see it in the hate.

Dee says God told her to do it. So in a deeply religious family, why hide that? God's will is followed in deeply religious families. If Dee felt she was doing what God wanted her to do, there should have been joy.

She committed the acts furtively because Dee knew that she was not obeying God. She was acting out of deep narcissistic anger at being trapped.

---

*No doubt Dee was influenced by a culture that does not value children.*

---

Though it is quite likely that Dee felt love for her children, she felt much more love for herself. She likely was ill equipped to spend her days alone, isolated, with three boys to care for and school.

## Our Culture Does Not Value Children

No doubt Dee was influenced by a culture that does not value children.

After all, we abort about a million a year. We allow a woman to prosecute a man for hitting her stomach during pregnancy, but that same woman can kill that same baby the next week if she gets tired of it.

We celebrate Laci and Conner's law to officially treat a fetus as a human, but say that another fetus can be plucked out when the woman fears a birth moment hangnail.

If all these things can be done to babies in America, but are not acceptable in a very religious wife and mother's world, imagine the anger a "religious" woman can build up toward children she does not really want.

And that is the gist of Dee's hate for her children. That they were there.

Parenting takes away a measure of freedom. Parents at some point have to put either their own or their children's needs first. Nature's way is that parents choose the welfare of the children. They give up their own youth, to move toward their own death. It is part of the maturation process of humans, and nature's way of marching humans through the years. Dee didn't like her fate, so she killed her children to get out of it.

Dee is reportedly on super suicide watch. She cries wrenchingly as the details of her actions are reported in court. Just as Andrea Yates did, a hauntingly similar case. But as time wore on in court, Andrea Yates began to look lighter and younger and happier. As no doubt Dee will.

Since sanity is tried in the courts and not in the counseling room, someone may finally speak for the dead children. They are the real victims. Dee has already gotten what she wanted. The children who were the focus of hate are gone.

# Hate Crime Laws Protect the Disabled

*Brian T. McMahon, Steven L. West, Allen N. Lewis, Amy J. Armstrong, and Joseph P. Conway*

*Brian T. McMahon is a professor in the Department of Physical Medicine and Rehabilitation Counseling at Virginia Commonwealth University (VCU), in Richmond, Virginia. Steven L. West, Allen N. Lewis, and Amy J. Armstrong are assistant professors of rehabilitation counseling at VCU. Joseph P. Conway is a doctoral candidate in allied health sciences at VCU.*

In September 1997, local police investigated an alleged sexual assault that had occurred behind a grocery store in Massachusetts. A 21-year-old woman with mild retardation reported that she had been duct-taped to a tree and molested, then sexually assaulted in a parked van and again in an empty building. The police arrested a 60-year-old local drifter and charged him with indecent assault and battery on a mentally retarded person—a crime punishable by up to 20 years in prison. The defense attorney on the case argued that the two were friends and that the sex was consensual. The man had no criminal history and was described as "slow," although he had no formal diagnosis of disability. The case resulted in a plea bargain involving 2 years' probation and no jail time.

In March 1998, another incident of rape of a woman with a disability was investigated in Massachusetts. The victim was a 36-year-old woman who used a wheelchair for mobility and had severe mental retardation and a severe speech impediment. She named a caretaker at her state-funded residence as the assailant. Because of her disabilities, authorities determined that the woman would be a liability in court. Conse-

Brian T. McMahon, Steven L. West, Allen N. Lewis, Amy J. Armstrong, and Joseph P. Conway, "Hate Crimes and Disability in America," *Rehabilitation Counseling Bulletin*, vol. 47, no. 2, Winter 2004, p. 66. Republished with permission from the publisher, conveyed through Copyright Clearance Center, Inc.

quently, there was no arrest, prosecution, or conviction. A detective assigned to the case reflected upon the difficulties in prosecuting cases in which victims' testimony would likely hurt their situations rather than help. Case closed.

## The Disabled Are Easy Victims

These scenarios illustrate a situation that is all too common for Americans with disabilities. Negative attitudes toward and stereotypes regarding people with disabilities result in experiences of marginalization, isolation, and victimization. Research indicates that individuals with disabilities experience a heightened risk of sexual, physical, and emotional abuse. For example, the threat of being physically or sexually assaulted is 4 to 10 times higher for adults with developmental disabilities than it is for other adults. . . .

---

*Indeed, that is the intent of hate crimes—not only to harm the victim but also to send a message of intimidation to an entire community.*

---

## Hate Crime Definition

An *attitude* is an emotionally charged idea that links particular actions to certain situations. Attitudes can be positive or negative. *Bias* is a preformed negative attitude toward a group based on race, religion, ethnicity/national origin, sexual orientation, or disability status. A *bias crime*, also known as a *hate crime*, is a criminal offense committed against person or property that is motivated, in whole or in part, by the offender's bias. An offense is still a bias crime even if the offender was mistaken in his or her perception that the victim was a member of the group he or she was acting against. With respect to disability, crimes motivated by hate victimize the individual and result in long-standing traumatic stress. Such crimes also send a violent shock rippling throughout the entire community of Americans with disabilities. Indeed, that is the intent of hate crimes—not only to harm the victim but also to send a message of intimidation to an entire community. . . .

Individuals with disabilities may be more vulnerable to crime and thus more likely to be victims of violent crimes. Three sets of contributory factors should be explored: situational context, personal features, and societal contributions. Certain situations foster isolation, dependence, and a genuine sense of vulnerability. Individuals with disabilities are more likely to live in poverty, with nearly 3 times as many having household incomes under $15,000 (29% vs. 10% for persons without disabilities). High levels of poverty translate directly to low levels of home ownership and higher levels of residence in rental housing, public housing, congregate living, and institutions. Less than one third of Americans with disabilities are competitively employed (32% vs. 81% labor force participation rate for persons without disabilities), and their labor force participation is characterized by part-time employment, a lack of benefits, and secondary labor market placements. Individuals with disabilities are more reliant upon public transportation with uneven levels of accessibility. Finally, this population often utilizes personal assistants or others for personal care, transportation, or communication, and these helpers have inconsistent levels of training, competence, and commitment.

Personal features related to the nature and severity of an individual's disability may also contribute to that person's vulnerability. For example, the lack of opportunity to develop social skills often results in social isolation and compliant personalities. Some disabilities involve an inability to comprehend the nature of criminal activities or the resources available for victim assistance. An individual may lack assertiveness or the sense of control or choice regarding personal affairs, or may feel he or she has no credibility when reporting a crime.

Disability advocates also explain vulnerability as a consequence of negative public attitudes (more acute among adolescents, who are more prone to violent activities). Inaccessible environments that inhibit escape, help-seeking, and reporting of crimes are primary impediments to full citizenship in the criminal justice arena.

## The Disabled Are a Protected Community

On April 23, 1990, President George H.W. Bush signed the Hate Crime Statistics Act, which requires the attorney general to collect data about crimes that manifest evidence of prejudice based on race, religion, sexual orientation, or ethnicity. On that date, criminal conduct became forever distinct when it involved an act of discrimination, and the law became one means to battle the violent manifestations of bigotry. The FBI Uniform Crime Reporting Section was given responsibility for data collection. After considering and rejecting a nationwide sampling approach, the FBI decided to incorporate hate crimes data into the established National Incident-Based Reporting System. This required adding a single new data element to flag a criminal incident as bias-motivated. When the Hate Crime Statistics Act was reauthorized in 1994, disability was added to the list of protected categories, for four reasons.

First, Americans with disabilities constitute a large group, estimated by some at 54 million citizens, although the current lack of reliable statistical data on disability prevalence is well documented. Second, Americans with disabilities seem to have some measure of collective identity. The third reason rests on the ample available evidence that illustrates a pattern of historical discrimination, which has taken the form of such acts as assisted suicide; sexual abuse in families; physical abuse in institutions; and "legitimate" medical practices, such as aversive conditioning, electroconvulsive therapy, psychosurgery, sterilization, medical experimentation, and excessive medication. So pervasive are discriminatory incidents that in a historical insight by Congress the "preamble" (purposes and findings) of the Americans with Disabilities Act (ADA) acknowledges "a history of purposeful unequal treatment . . . [against] a discrete and insular minority who have been . . . relegated to a position of political powerlessness in our society."

The fourth and most compelling reason is the enactment of the ADA. This landmark civil rights act infused disability as a standard subject in federal discrimination law. It is interesting to note that inclusion of other specific groups in hate crimes legislation (e.g., children, the elderly, police officers, union members) was expressly denied. By contrast, no congressional hearing was held on violence directed at persons with disability, yet no objection was heard regarding their inclusion. . . .

Hate crimes can have dual intent—animus *and* actuarial.[1] They can also be staged to conceal the motivation of bias. Over time, the courts have maintained that what really matters is that a victim was selected "because of" his or her status (disability, even if the perception is that disability implies vulnerability). However, at the level of policing (where original classification of hate crimes occurs), a distinction is made regarding actuarial considerations. The courts and police may be using different standards in classifying hate crimes, and as long as police require the more stringent "symbolic" definition, then hate crimes against Americans with disabilities will continue to be grossly undercounted.

The issue of vulnerability, real or perceived, may explain in part the "actuarial" motivation of perpetrators for crimes "of opportunity." This interpretation by police, which is embedded in training and at odds with the courts, helps explain the failure of thousands of hate crimes to be properly classified as such. For reasons already provided, self-reporting of

---

1. Some hate crimes are committed with the intent of expressing animus or hate toward a particular group. "Actuarial" crimes are those in which the perpetrator chooses victims because they look vulnerable, not because they belong to a given social category.

hate crimes by Americans with disabilities is challenging enough without institutional impediments in the criminal justice system that discourage or inhibit both reporting and prosecution of crimes against Americans with disabilities.

# Hate Crime Laws May Hurt Minorities

*Phyllis B. Gerstenfeld*

*Phyllis B. Gerstenfeld chairs the Department of Sociology and Criminal Justice at California State University–Stanislaus. Her areas of research include hate crimes, juvenile justice, the Internet and criminal justice, and psychology and the law. She is the author of* Hate Crimes: Causes, Controls, and Controversies.

Most advocates of hate crime legislation are genuinely concerned with the insidious effects of bigotry and see these laws as a viable and even necessary means of combating those effects. Many critics of the laws share the same concerns, but some of them worry that hate crime laws might actually result in the paradoxical effect of harming members of minority groups.

## Hate Crime Laws May Inspire Complacency

One way that hate crime laws might be counterproductive is that they might inspire complacency among policymakers. By the relatively simple act of enacting hate crime legislation, politicians may feel that they have done their part to combat prejudice. It is politically expedient for them to pass this legislation: They can satisfy civil rights activists while simultaneously appearing tough on crime. And advocacy groups might also find themselves so busy addressing the relatively rare problem of hate-motivated crime that they largely overlook the much more common (albeit subtle) problems of bias in employment, education, housing, and other facets of everyday life. This dilemma is made worse by the fact that hate crime laws will probably have very little direct effect on hate.

[Susan] Gellman is one author who has made this point:

> If enacting a largely ineffective ethnic intimidation statute allows us to feel that we have taken steps to eliminate bigotry and bias-related crime and thus reduces somewhat or even entirely our feeling of the urgency of doing more, the enactment of the law ultimately *slows* the process of combating bigotry.

---

*A second risk of hate crime laws is that they will inspire resentment of minorities.*

---

Some empirical evidence supports this argument. [Researchers Sarah A.] Soule and [Jennifer S.] Earle found that states that had initially enacted hate crime data collection or civil legislation were significantly slower to adopt hate crime laws. These authors refer to this as a "buffer" effect and conclude that "data collection and private civil redress statutes, when unaccompanied by criminalization, serve to deflect pressure for hate crime laws while not actually providing important protections for potential hate crime victims". . .

## Hate Crime Laws Create Resentment

A second risk of hate crime laws is that they will inspire resentment of minorities. This phenomenon is similar to the way in which children often dislike the "teacher's pet". Members of the general public, who are usually uninformed about the realities of how the laws work, may feel that certain groups are getting special treatment.

White supremacist groups appear to be taking advantage of this angle. Several of their Web sites, for example, state (incorrectly) that the laws protect only minorities, not white people. Some of them claim that the laws result in the persecution of white Christians. Some also decry what they call the "real" hate crimes—crimes committed by blacks against whites—and claim that the government and the media are ignoring those happenings. It is unclear how many people are actually convinced by this rhetoric, but the extremist groups seem to think it is worth their while to post these messages.

A third, more troubling possibility is that hate crime laws could be used to disempower minorities. The government is hardly a neutral bystander when it comes to bias; in fact, it has a long history of perpetuating and encouraging bias. . . .

Lest this sound like radicalism or some sort of conspiracy theory, consider historical events. For example, in 1956, the Alabama Attorney General used state incorporation requirements to attempt to oust the NAACP [National Association for the Advancement of Colored People] from Alabama. The Attorney General enjoyed 8 years of success in the courts in this endeavor until the U.S. Supreme Court finally ruled the effort unconstitutional (*NAACP v. Alabama*, 1964). Alabama also tried to require the NAACP to turn over the names and addresses of all its members (*NAACP v. Alabama*, 1958). Also in 1956, Louisiana tried to expel the NAACP via the state laws on registering organizations (ultimately, the state failed, *Gremillion v. NAACP*, 1961). In 1957, Virginia sought to use its statutes prohibiting solicitation by lawyers to restrain the NAACP from providing legal assistance in civil rights cases (this was also held unconstitutional in *NAACP v. Button*, 1963).

Clearly, states have not hesitated to use what appear to be neutral statutes to try to weaken individuals or groups who question the status quo. Had hate crime statutes existed during the 1960s, is it not possible that civil rights activists could have been charged with hate crimes? After all, is not a sit-in at a segregated lunch counter arguably a trespass committed because of race?

## Hate Crime Laws Can Disempower Minorities

Again, there is some empirical support for the argument that hate crime laws could be used to disempower members of minority groups. Official hate crime data have consistently shown that, although African Americans are disproportionately likely to be the victims of hate crimes, they are also disproportionately likely to be identified as the perpetrators. For example, in Minnesota, approximately 2.2% of the population is African American. In 1993, however, 36.9% of the reported hate crime victims were black, as were 34% of the reported offenders. In 2000, according to the FBI, 18.7% of the offenders were black; about 12% of the United States population is African American.

---

*A final risk of hate crime laws is that, rather than reducing prejudice through their symbolic message, they will actually increase it.*

---

The reasons for this pattern are unclear. It is possible that, due to factors such as economic deprivation and anger over racism, blacks actually do commit more hate crimes. On the other hand, it is possible that victims, witnesses, and police officers are more likely to interpret a crime as hate motivated when the offender is white than when he is black. It could also be a statistical fluke: Because whites are the majority in most places, a person of any race who chooses a crime victim at random is probably going to choose a white victim. Incidents between a white offender and white victim are unlikely to be interpreted as hate crimes, whereas those between a black offender and a white victim might. Whatever the explanation (and, clearly, this issue merits more research), this is a troubling trend. . . .

## The Risk of More Prejudice

A final risk of hate crime laws is that, rather than reducing prejudice through their symbolic message, they will actually increase it. On the level of the individual offender, this seems quite likely; a defendant will probably not reform his or her bigoted ways after being convicted of a hate crime. To the contrary, the conviction may actually increase his or her standing among peers by making him or her into a martyr and a hero. The perpetrator may also blame the group to which the victim belongs—after all, if it were not for that group, he or she would not have been found guilty of a crime. Moreover, incarcerating a racist will hardly reform him or her. Prisons and jails are among the most prejudice-ridden institutions in our society. Prison gangs are usually organized along racial and ethnic lines, and they sometimes have ties to external extremist organizations.

On a larger scale, it is questionable whether hate crime laws will reduce prejudice in the community in general. Two psychological theories might predict the opposite. First, the theory of attitudinal inoculation predicts that if people have never been exposed to weak counterarguments to beliefs they hold, they are especially vulnerable to strong arguments later. It is akin to being vaccinated: Initial exposure to a weak form of the virus provides resistance to the virus in its full form. Hate crime laws might discourage people from openly expressing biased beliefs. People who never hear these types of beliefs might later fall under the influence of a particularly persuasive, bigoted speaker.

# Hate Crime Laws
# Are Unconstitutional

*Susan B. Gellman*

*Susan B. Gellman is a private attorney with the law firm of Wolman and Genshaft in Columbus, Ohio. She is also the vice chair of the First Amendment Rights Committee, Individual Rights and Responsibilities Section of the American Bar Association.*

Proponents of bias-crime laws have the best of intentions, but these laws, in the end, create thought crimes. As used here, "bias-crime law" refers to the common hate-crime statute (also commonly referred to as a "bump-up" statute) that enhances the penalty and/or grade of an already existing offense if the offense was motivated by bias. The statute establishes one penalty for the underlying crime—assault or vandalism for instance—and another penalty for the defendant's bigotry that motivated the offense.

The legislatures enacting these statutes are targeting bigoted, hateful thought, and the special harms that crimes associated with those thoughts are, reasonably, said to cause. The government's decision to take bigotry seriously and express disapproval of it is commendable. The idea was that although the First Amendment prevents punishment of having or expressing bigoted thoughts, there would be no problem punishing the thought if it were coupled with conduct, conduct that is itself already a crime.

But that is precisely the problem with these statutes: they punish defendants once for what they have done, and once for having had a government-disapproved thought. Thought or opinion that is not punishable on its own does not become

Susan B. Gellman, "Agreeing to Agree: A Proponent and Opponent of Hate Crime Laws Reach for Common Ground," *Harvard Journal of Legislation*, vol. 41, no. 2, Summer 2004, pp. 425–28, 432–33. Reproduced by permission.

punishable when it accompanies criminal conduct. The accompanying criminal conduct does not work some special alchemy to change the reality that there is an additional penalty—sometimes as large or even much larger than the penalty for the base crime—imposed solely for the bigoted thoughts.

These statutes are not only content-based, they are viewpoint-based. The statutes are even-handed in the sense that they punish bias regardless of whether it is, say, anti-black or anti-white. At the same time, however, they do take sides on a political and social issue: the extra punishment is imposed only for the bigoted viewpoint, not the anti-bigoted viewpoint. For example, if a racist threatens an African American by reason of the victim's race, the extra penalty applies, but if a non-racist onlooker then threatens the racist, there is no extra penalty.

## Purpose and Intent

It is true that the legal system does upgrade and even define certain offenses on the basis of purpose and intent. Those are—like motive—mental processes, so if purpose and intent constitute a permissible basis for punishment, proponents argue, motive can as well. Yet the law has long distinguished between purpose and intent, which determine what the offender is doing, and motive, which explains only why the offender is doing it. The children of a wealthy father may have a motive to kill him but no intent to do so; a psychopath may have no motive to kill but intend to do so anyway. A purpose or intent is not an opinion on a social or political issue; bigotry (the motive for bias crimes), noxious though it may be, is. Intent and purpose are punishable only when coupled with conduct, not because they are protected by the First Amendment, but because they are inchoate. With the actual commission of an act, however, their inchoate quality disappears, and there is no bar to their punishment—that is, to punish intentional or purposeful conduct more harshly than conduct that is accidental. The same is not true of bigoted motive, because of the constitutional bar to punishing opinion, even when associated with unlawful conduct.

## Bigotry Is Not a Crime

Many proponents of bias-crime laws are strong supporters of civil liberties. This has always been almost entirely a "liberal vs. liberal" debate. Proponents—to their credit—care so deeply about the problems of bigotry and bigotry-related crimes that when what seemed like a simple solution was proposed, they were too eager to convince themselves that the First Amendment presented no bar. The undercurrent seems to be a feeling that bigotry is special, so abhorrent that it is fitting for the government to treat it as criminal in itself.

People feel strongly that many other ideas are just as "wrong" and therefore deserving of special treatment. Occasionally, the Supreme Court agrees, and carves out a new category of so-called "unprotected" speech. But those cases are extremely rare, and fortunately so. In any case, the Supreme Court has never created an unprotected class of speech—as it did for obscenity and fighting words—for bigotry. Most likely, it is prevented from doing so by the First Amendment, just as it could not carve out exceptions for anti-American or blasphemous speech. In any event, until such time as the Supreme Court carves out such a class, if ever, government punishment of bigoted thoughts, even when accompanied by a crime, is constitutionally no different from government punishment of any other thought or opinion.

Punishment of conduct, verbal or otherwise, for a bigoted viewpoint poses the identical problem. It is likely few proponents of bias-crime laws would think that a law increasing penalties for crimes committed "by reason of the offender's support of the war" or "by reason of anti-Americanism" would be constitutional. And by this rationale, what would stop a state with a pro-choice majority from enhancing penalties for crimes committed "by reason of opposition to a woman's right to choose" while a neighboring state enhanced penalties for crimes committed "by reason of promotion of the taking of innocent human life"? Once a motive that represents an opinion or belief on any social or political belief can be criminalized, so can any of the above examples. . . .

---

*Thinking, believing, even hating, is simply not something government can punish.*

---

## Hateful Thought Is Not Illegal

It is quite an assumption that one could adequately prove that bias crimes always (or even likely) cause greater harm than crimes motivated by other motives such as greed, personal hatred, and political terrorism. It does not seem impossible, however, and the notion feels right intuitively, so let us assume that they do. In that case, it seems both logical and permissible to punish bias crimes more heavily, the same way that the Constitution permits more severe punishment of an assault that causes serious physical harm than one that does not.

There is a problem with that analogy, though, and it makes all the difference. Unlike the serious versus the minor physical assault, the greater harm caused by a hate-motivated crime is solely the effect of the offender's beliefs and/or expression of belief. In a case such as this, the extra harm is caused solely by the part of the offender's conduct that is pure First Amendment activity. Thinking, believing, even hating, is simply not something government can punish.

Most often, opponents of bias-crime legislation not only often concede, but affirmatively agree that hateful ideas and their expression cause real harm. In fact, the expression of hateful ideas causes harm whether it is accompanied by criminal conduct, non-criminal conduct, or no conduct at all.

Sometimes that extra harm amounts to offense, which, even in the case of deeply painful offense, is not punishable under the Constitution. Other times, though, the harm is more than offense: "terror" might be the best word for that harm (in the sense of great fear, rather than connection to political terrorism). But that same fear also arises without an accompanying criminal act. For example, how might you feel upon seeing someone merely reading a copy of *Mein Kampf* or a Ku Klux Klan newsletter? Surely, though, the proponents of bias-crime laws do not approve banning reading or writing, let alone believing, hateful messages, despite the harm the ideas and their expression do cause. The First Amendment forbids punishing the expression of thought, even hateful and harmful thought. That restriction on government power does not evaporate magically when the expression of hateful thought is accompanied by some punishable conduct.

## Upholding the First Amendment

What is left then but a symbolic effect? Bias-crimes laws arguably (although not demonstrably) make it slightly less politically correct to express bigotry. Even assuming there is any such shaming effect on anyone who would commit a bias crime, there are far more effective ways than criminalizing bigotry through bias-crime laws to accomplish this, either through government action or, better, socially. Certainly a criminal statute that does not infringe on First Amendment rights would make this symbolic statement at least as well. The criminal code is too clumsy a tool for social change generally, let alone such an easy, cheap, and politically popular quick-fix as passing bias-crime laws. It is *worse* when a statute is merely a symbolic gesture from the legislature that is then used as a cover for avoiding more difficult, and probably more expensive, action toward true equality. As James Jacobs and Kimberly Potter [authors of *Hate Crimes: Criminal Law and Identity Politics*] explained, "[H]ate crime laws may substitute for true 'institution building' in the area of community relations. Effectively, politicians may be getting off the hook too easily. Throwing laws at a problem costs no money and requires no political energy."

The effects of bigotry and bigoted expression are certainly more than offensive. Still, we should not whack at the First Amendment, even a little bit, for the sake of letting government officials pose for the cameras as they "make a tough statement about hate and violence in our communities" —and then go home.

# Federal Hate Crime Laws Will Not Reduce Violence

*Jeff Miller*

*U.S. representative Jeff Miller is a third-term Congressman from Florida. In 2005 Congressman Miller was appointed chair of the Veteran's Affairs Subcommittee on Disability Assistance and Memorial Affairs.*

*[Editor's Note: The following viewpoint is an excerpt of testimony delivered to Congress by Jeff Miller in opposition to the Conyers amendment to H.R. 3132, the bill making hate crimes a federal offense. In September 2005 the U.S. House of Representatives overwhelmingly passed H.R. 3132. The measure has been referred to the U.S. Senate.]*

M r. Speaker, this afternoon, the House passed an amended version of H.R. 3132, The Children's Safety Act of 2005. The bill as sent to the floor by the Judiciary Committee represented a tough crackdown on pedophilia and other sex offenses. The bill modifies the national sex offender registration program, expands the use of DNA to identify and prosecute sex offenders, increases penalties for sexual offenses against America's children, and makes other much-needed modifications and expansions of federal law relating to child safety.

Before the bill passed, however, an amendment by Rep. John Conyers (D-MI) was added, drastically altering this bill. I voted against the Conyers amendment, and its passage forced me to vote against final passage of the bill.

The Conyers amendment creates a Federal offense for hate crimes. I believe that the proponents of hate crimes legislation have good and honorable intentions. They would like to see

Jeff Miller, Congressional Record—Extensions of Remarks, U.S. House of Representatives, September 14, 2005, pp. E1850–51.

less bigotry and more good will in American society. While I share that goal, I believe Congress should decline the invitation to enact hate crimes legislation for both constitutional and practical reasons.

The U.S. Constitution created a federal government of limited powers. Most of the federal government's "delegated powers" are set forth in Article I, Section 8. The Tenth Amendment was added to make it clear that the powers not delegated to the federal government "are reserved to the States respectively, or to the people."

Crime is a serious problem, but under the U.S. Constitution it is a matter to be handled by state and local government. In recent years, Congress has federalized the crimes of gun possession within a school zone, carjacking, and wife beating. All of that and more has been rationalized under the Commerce Clause [which regulates interstate commerce]. The Commerce Clause is not a blank check for Congress to enact whatever legislation it deems to be "good and proper for America." The Conyers Amendment is simply beyond the powers that are delegated to Congress. Today, the House exacerbated the errors of past Congresses by federalizing more criminal offenses

---

*Hate crime laws are unnecessary in the first place.*

---

Not to mention the fact that the Conyers language isn't going to prevent anything. Any thug that is already inclined to hurt another human being is not going to lay down the gun or knife because of some new law passed by Congress; they've already made a conscious decision to disregard basic homicide statutes. The notion that any federal hate crime law will prevent brutal killings is preposterous.

For the proponents of hate crime laws, the dilemma is this: if some groups (women, gays, vegans, runners, whatever) are left out of the "hate crime" definition, they will resent the selective depreciation of their victimization. On the other hand, if all victim groups are included, the hate crime category will be no different than "ordinary" criminal law.

Federalizing hate crime law will not increase tolerance in our society or reduce intergroup conflict. I believe hate crime laws may well have the opposite effect. The men and women who will be administering the hate crime laws (e.g. police, prosecutors) will likely encounter a never-ending series of complaints with respect to their official decisions. When a U.S. Attorney declines to prosecute a certain offense as a hate crime, some will complain that he is favoring the groups to which the accused belongs (e.g. Hispanic males). And when a U.S. Attorney does prosecute an offense as a hate crime, some will complain that the decision was based upon politics and that the government is favoring the groups to which the victim belongs (e.g. Asian Americans).

Perhaps the most dangerous element of federalized hate crime law is its approach to the notion of thought crimes. But once hate crime laws are on the books, the law enforcement apparatus will be delving into the accused's life and thoughts in order to show that he or she was motivated by bigotry. What kind of books and magazines were found in the home? What internet sites were bookmarked in the computer? Friends and coworkers will be interviewed to discern the accused's politics and worldview. The point here is that such chilling examples of state intrusion are avoidable because, as noted above, hate crime laws are unnecessary in the first place.

## The Law Does Not Protect Children

But above all else, I cannot comprehend why anyone would believe that the Conyers hate crimes language makes our children any safer from sexual predators. . . .

Our children deserve strong anti-pedophilia laws that meet basic constitutional thresholds and it's our responsibility to deliver that to them.

# Hate Crime Laws Create a Double Standard

*Jeff Jacoby*

*Jeff Jacoby is an op-ed newspaper columnist for the* Boston Globe. *He is also on the board of the* Concord Review, *a quarterly journal of essays on history by high-school students around the world.*

They were crimes that shocked the nation. On 7 June 1998, three white ex-convicts in Jasper, Texas chained a forty-nine-year-old black hitchhiker to the back of a pickup truck and dragged him down a rough rural road to his death, his mutilated body parts leaving a trail nearly three miles long.

Four months later, in Laramie, Wyoming, a young gay man was lured from a student bar, driven out of town, beaten with a blunt instrument until his skull collapsed, hog-tied to a fence, and left for dead.

The murders of James Byrd Jr. and Matthew Shepard scandalized and horrified Americans. Each drew enormous media attention and each was promptly seized upon as proof of the need for more and stronger laws to punish 'hate crimes'. Violence that stems from bigotry and intolerance, it was said, is worse than other kinds of violence. In President Bill Clinton's words: 'Crimes that are motivated by hate really are fundamentally different and I believe should be treated differently under the law.'

## Hate Crime Laws Are Ultimately Harmful

It is an argument that has met with much success. By 1998 hate crime legislation—laws increasing the punishment for a

Jeff Jacoby, *The Hate Debate: Should Hate Be Punished as a Crime?* London: Institute for Jewish Policy Research, 2002, pp. 114–22. Copyright © 2002, Institute for Jewish Policy Research. Reproduced by permission.

given crime when the offender acted out of certain specified types of prejudice or bigotry—was in force in 41 of the 50 US states. Limited hate crime laws were in force at the federal level, too: the Hate Crimes Sentencing Enhancement Act and the Violence Against Women Act, for example. In 2000 and 2001 the US Senate (although not the House of Representatives) voted to expand sharply the federal government's authority to prosecute crimes stemming from bias, and to reach not only crimes based on race, colour, religion or national origin, but those motivated by the victim's sexual orientation or disability as well.

Notwithstanding their popularity, hate crime laws are badly misguided. The assumptions on which they are based do not stand up to scrutiny. And their ultimate effect will be to cause more damage than they prevent.

---

*It is unjust and indecent for the statute books to enshrine a double standard that makes some victims more equal than others.*

---

Hate crime laws are grounded in the conviction that attacks motivated by bigotry are more damaging than attacks stemming from other motivations. Certainly it is bad to be beaten by an attacker because he wants your money, the advocates of these laws say, but it is worse to be beaten by an attacker because he hates people of your colour or religion or sexual orientation. And, since a worse crime deserves a worse punishment, it is appropriate to increase the penalties meted out for hate crimes.

But is the premise really true? *Is* bigotry a more reprehensible motive than greed? Than lust? Than ideology? Than a desire to humiliate? It is hardly obvious that a hit-man who murders for money or a serial killer who does it for a thrill poses less of a threat to society—and therefore deserves less of a punishment—than someone who murders out of prejudice.

# Hate Crime Laws Treat Victims Differently

Hate crime laws declare, in effect, that the blood of a man attacked by a bigot is redder than that of a man attacked by a sadist or a thief. But what is the case for saying so? Do the children of a man murdered because he was black grieve less than the children of a man murdered because he had $50 in his pocket? Does the victim suffer less? If James Byrd had been dragged to his death by three black men, would his murder have been any less monstrous? In a society dedicated to the ideal of 'equal justice under law'—the words are engraved over the entrance to the Supreme Court in Washington, DC—it is unjust and indecent for the statute books to enshrine a double standard that makes some victims more equal than others.

Typically, supporters of hate crime laws justify the added penalties by claiming that the attacks cause added harm. 'Hate crimes are a form of terrorism,' said Senator Edward Kennedy of Massachusetts at a legislative hearing in 1998. 'They have a psychological and emotional impact which extends far beyond the victim. They threaten the entire community, and undermine the ideals on which the nation was founded.' Professor Kent Greenawalt of the Columbia University Law School makes a similar point: 'Such crimes can frighten and humiliate other members of the community; they can also reinforce social divisions and hatred.'

These observations are true, of course. But they are true of all violent crime. Every murder, every rape, every mugging victimizes more people than just the victim him/herself. That is one reason criminal prosecutions are always conducted in the name of the citizenry: *People v. Gacy, United States v. McVeigh, Commonwealth v. O'Neill.*

No reasonable person would deny that a violent crime committed against a member of a minority group can strike terror in the hearts of other members of that group. But non-hate crimes can do so as well. The kidnapping and murder of a child, the rape of a jogger in a public park, a drive-by gang shooting, the mugging of an elderly woman: don't these too 'have a psychological and emotional impact which extends far beyond the victim' to 'threaten the entire community'? It is not easy to see why the fear and menace felt by one segment of society—Jews, say, or Blacks—warrant the imposition of an extra-severe sentence while the fear and menace felt by another segment—senior citizens or residents of public housing or parents—don't.

## Hate Crimes Create a Double Standard

Hate crime laws create an indefensible double standard. There is no way around it: a statute that imposes harsher penalties for hurting certain kinds of people proclaims by definition that hurting other kinds of people isn't quite as bad. Thugs who like to beat up Jews or Hispanics are on notice that the criminal code will increase their sentence if they are prosecuted and convicted. Thugs who like to beat up fat people—or socialists or businessmen or redheads or football fans—can do so with greater impunity. *Those* groups don't enjoy special protection.

Although most of the US states had enacted hate crime laws by 1998, two of those that hadn't were the ones where Byrd and Shepard were lynched: Texas and Wyoming. If they had, it was suggested, things would have been different. 'His death', editorialized the *New York Times* after Shepard was killed, 'makes clear the need for hate-crime laws to protect those who survive and punish those who attack others, whether fatally or not, just because of who they are'.

Likewise, Byrd's murder was cited as proof of the need for a tougher federal hate crime law. 'A strong response is clearly needed,' said Senator Kennedy not long after the killing in Jasper. To drive home the point, Byrd's daughter was brought to Washington to testify in the bill's favour.

## Hate Crime Laws Are Not a Deterrent

But what difference could another hate crime law—state *or* federal—have possibly made? 'A strong response'? Of the three men who killed Byrd, two were sentenced to death and one is to spend the rest of his life behind bars. How much stronger a response did Kennedy have in mind? Shepard's killers, too, were sentenced to life imprisonment. One of them, Aaron McKinney, was facing a death sentence when Shepard's parents proposed a deal: two life sentences in exchange for a permanent gag order preventing McKinney from ever appealing the verdict or discussing the case in public. What could a hate crime law have done that the existing murder law didn't do?

---

*The push for hate crime laws is fuelled by the belief that crimes based on hate have reached epidemic proportions.*

---

'I'm convinced', Kennedy said at another hearing in 1999, that 'if Congress acted today, and President Clinton signed our bill tomorrow, we'd have fewer hate crimes in all the days that follow.' But this is specious. There is no state where prosecutors would ignore a monstrous violent crime or fail to demand a harsh punishment. Everything the murderers in Jasper and Laramie did—kidnapping, aggravated robbery, assault, murder—is already a crime in every US state and in every civilized country. Existing law provides harsh punishments. All that is necessary is to enforce the statutes already on the books.

## Hate Crimes Have Not Reached Epidemic Proportions

The push for hate crime laws is fuelled by the belief that crimes based on hate have reached epidemic proportions. 'It has become nearly impossible to keep track of the shocking rise in brutal attacks directed against individuals *because* they are black, Latino, Asian, white, disabled, women, or gay,' write

sociologists Jack Levin and Jack McDevitt in their 1993 book
*Hate Crimes: The Rising Tide of Bigotry and Bloodshed.*

> Almost daily, the newspapers report new and even more
> grotesque abominations. . . . As ugly as this situation is now,
> it is likely to worsen throughout the remainder of the de-
> cade and into the next century as the forces of bigotry con-
> tinue to gain momentum.

The same claim has been made repeatedly by politicians, schol-
ars and various racial, religious and sexual activist organizations—and then amplified and re-broadcast by the media.

In the best book yet published on the subject—*Hate
Crimes: Criminal Law and Identity Politics* (1998)—James B.
Jacobs and Kimberly Potter round up an extraordinary collec-
tion of the alarmist rhetoric to which Americans have been
exposed in recent years. Some sample headlines: A CANCER
OF HATRED AFFLICTS AMERICA; RISE IN HATE CRIMES
SIGNALS ALARMING RESURGENCE OF BIGOTRY; BLACK-
ON-WHITE HATE CRIMES RISING; DECADE ENDED IN
BLAZE OF HATE; COMBATING HATE: CRIMES AGAINST
MINORITIES ARE INCREASING ACROSS THE BOARD.

But dig into the statistics, and these turn out to be wild
exaggerations. Hate 'crimes' are often not much more than incidents; in the FBI's official statistics, 'intimidation' is the most
common offence, while the absolute number of violent bias
crimes identified by the FBI is minuscule. Politicians, journalists and advocates find the notion of a hate crime 'epidemic'
irresistible, perhaps because it is easier to denounce bigotry
than to confront seriously violent crime in general. But the
data are clear: of the roughly 20,000 homicides, 30,000 rapes,
150,000 robberies and half a million aggravated assaults for
which police will make arrests in the United States this year,
only the tiniest fraction would qualify as hate crimes. Nothing
is gained by shining a spotlight on that fraction and eclipsing
the rest.

## Hate Crimes Criminalize Opinions

One of the worst defects of hate crime laws is that they punish not just deeds, but opinions: not just what the criminal did, but what he believed. This amounts to an assault on freedom of speech and belief, and ought to have no part in the criminal justice system of a liberal democracy.

'There is no such crime as a crime of thought,' the renowned defence lawyer Clarence Darrow once said 'there are only crimes of action'. In a free society, everyone is allowed to think bad thoughts and hold pernicious points of view. But contemporary hate crime laws turn those thoughts and points of view into crimes themselves. Certain states of mind, they declare, are so objectionable, so intolerable, that anyone who acts on them deserves especially severe punishment. Defenders of hate crime statutes argue that it is not the state of mind that is being punished, it is the crime it led to. But when the judge can send you to prison for an additional ten years because the aggravated assault you committed was motivated by your bigoted opinion of the victim, it is hard to reach any conclusion but the obvious one: your opinion has been criminalized.

'Thought crime', George Orwell called it in *Nineteen Eighty-Four*. A government that can punish you for your unorthodox thoughts about Blacks or Jews or homosexuals is that much closer to being able to punish you for your unorthodox thoughts about anything else. That is a prospect that should alarm any citizen who treasures his liberty.

> *Hate crime laws ... declare that some victims are more deserving than others. That is a message no citizen should be willing to accept.*

## Hate Laws Are Divisive

In an age when citizens are under constant pressure to splinter into groups—to see themselves first and foremost as members of an aggrieved race, class or gender—the last thing they need are more laws emphasizing their differences and calling inordinate attention to bias and hatred. Hate crime laws further a deeply destructive trend: an insistence on casting violent offenders not merely as criminals who threaten society's well-being, but as various kinds of bigots: racists, sexists, gay-bashers, Jew-haters. This is profoundly wrong. The purpose of criminal law is not to protect Blacks from Whites, Jews from neo-Nazis, women from misogynists, gays from straights, or immigrants from nativists. It is to protect all of us from law-breakers.

Every offence covered by a hate crime law was illegal to begin with. Each one could have been prosecuted under the existing criminal code. It may sound admirable to talk of 'preventing hate crimes' with new laws, but such laws prevent nothing except social unity. What they promote is balkanization, class warfare and identity politics.

Equal protection under law is the ideal of every democratic society. A government that takes that ideal seriously tells potential criminals that they will be punished fully and fairly, regardless of the identity of their victims. Hate crime laws, by contrast, declare that some victims are more deserving than others. That is a message no citizen should be willing to accept.

CHAPTER 3

# Should Hate Speech Be Restricted?

# Chapter Preface

The First Amendment of the United States Constitution provides that "Congress shall make no law ... abridging the freedom of speech, or of the press." However, the U.S. Supreme Court has carved out some exceptions over the years, meaning that the First Amendment provides less than full protection to commercial speech, defamation, speech that may be harmful to children, speech broadcast on radio and television, and public employees' speech. These exceptions to not include hate speech because the constitution fully protects speech that some may find offensive, unpopular, or even racist.

Unlike America, Europe does not have a strong free-speech tradition and hate speech is increasingly being criminalized. Since the 1970s Europe has been passing bans on speech that incites hatred based on race, religion, ethnicity, and national origin. These laws were broadened during the 1980s and 1990s in the face of rising violence against minorities. For example, a 1972 French law prohibiting Holocaust denial was recently expanded to include points of view deemed racist. In February 2006, Great Britain amended a 1986 racial hatred incitement law to criminalize intentionally "stirring up hatred against persons on religious grounds." The outlawing of hate speech is spreading throughout the entire European Union. Rules have been implemented to prohibit the broadcast, including online, of any program or advertisement that incites "hatred based on sex, race or ethnic origin, religion or belief, disability, age, or sexual orientation or is offensive to religious or political beliefs." These anti-incitement laws are problematic because increasingly they are used to threaten and intimidate people who are well within the political mainstream. Political speech is thus stunted as ordinary people are forced to censor themselves or face heavy fines and possible incarceration.

# The Majority of Americans Support Campus Hate Speech Codes

*Jon B. Gould*

*Jon. B. Gould is assistant professor in the Department of Public and International Affairs at George Mason University in Fairfax, Virginia.*

The new millennium has seen another organized attack against college hate speech policies, this time by the Foundation for Individual Rights in Education (FIRE). Led by its founders Alan Kors and Harvey Silverglate, FIRE in 2003 successfully challenged Shippensburg University in Pennsylvania for a speech policy that, according to FIRE, chilled the rights of students "to freely and openly engage in appropriate discussions of their theories, ideas and political and/or religious beliefs." The suit presaged FIRE's launch of Speechcodes.org, a Web site that purported to "catalog speech codes at public and private colleges and universities across the country." According to FIRE, the lawsuit and new Web site represent an "unprecedented national campaign that will end—through legal action and through public exposure—the scandal of unconstitutional censorship at America's public college and university campuses and that will force private institutions to choose between liberty and tyranny."

FIRE is not alone in contesting college hate speech regulation. In 2001, conservative activist David Horowitz crafted a highly controversial advertisement against reparations for slavery and sent the ad to a selection of newspapers at the most prestigious and liberal colleges across the country. The ad drew a firestorm of protest at many schools, with several

Jon B. Gould, from *Speak No Evil: The Triumph of Hate Speech Regulation.* University of Chicago Press, 2005, pp. 173–78. Copyright © 2005 by the University of Chicago. All rights reserved. Reproduced by permission.

newspapers refusing to run the ad and others apologizing to their readers for having inflamed the campus community. Despite his protestations to the contrary—according to Horowitz "this kind of censorship . . . should send chills up anybody's spine"—Horowitz appeared delighted with the response. Known as a "rightist rabble-rouser," Horowitz used the controversy to jump-start his "'Freedom Tour' of campus lectures," reveling, as he said, in "my 15 minutes of fame."

FIRE is correct that many schools still retain their hate speech policies, some of them challenging or even overstepping constitutional norms. . . . [An examination] of 100 schools . . . finds that most still have the same speech rules on the books in 2004 that they maintained seven years earlier. But this fact does not tell the whole story, for FIRE's claims are by turns both too broad and too narrow. FIRE has taken to rating college speech policies, claiming that upwards of two-thirds of public campuses have unconstitutional policies. This number, however, is an exaggeration. Among other things FIRE does not distinguish between enforceable rules and exhortative statements; it confuses examples with definitions; and it takes statements out of context.

A good example is FIRE's charge that the University of Michigan's Policy and Guidelines Regarding Electronic Access to Potentially Offensive Material is unconstitutional for stating that "individuals should not be unwittingly exposed to offensive material by the deliberate and knowing acts of others." At best this line is ambiguous—the debate being whether the policy is restricting expression that the offender knows is offensive or material that the offender believes a recipient would find offensive. The context of the policy, however, should answer this question in favor of Michigan, especially considering that the policy applies only to computer systems administrators, not to students or faculty. More shocking is FIRE's exclusion of a line in the policy that clearly supports free speech and open expression: "[S]ystem administrators will have to guard against making judgments as to the appropriateness of the content of another person's work. Research and instruction take many forms and may not be restricted through censorship." Indeed, such luminaries as Robert O'Neil, director of the Thomas Jefferson Center for the Protection of Free Expression and former president of the University of Virginia, have contested FIRE's claims and estimates. Says O'Neil, "I just can't believe there are anything like that number of genuine speech codes."

---

*Hate speech restrictions are increasingly the norm among influential institutions of civil society, including higher education, the news media, and Internet service providers.*

---

## FIRE Has Lost the War

For all its focus on the precise number of college hate speech policies, FIRE risks missing the larger point that it is losing the war over hate speech regulation in general. Rather than being considered an unconstitutional pariah, hate speech restrictions are increasingly the norm among influential institutions of civil society, including higher education, the news media, and Internet service providers. Even as FIRE and its compatriots have won legal battles in court, the informal law of speech regulation has prospered. This, then, is the ultimate irony; adopted largely for utilitarian or instrumental purposes, the speech codes have had the very effect on mass constitutionalism and speech norms that their opponents originally feared. Without a court case won or a statute passed, the bounds of free speech have been reinterpreted and a new norm spread in civil society.

Initially, some of the evidence may appear to the contrary. Throughout the qualitative research I found few schools that had actively enforced their hate speech policies, the highest rate constituting one case per year. Part of the reason, says a former college president, is that "adopting policies is easier than acting on actual cases. . . . Policies are non-action," which most college administrators prefer, he says. "Usually, the least action a president can take is to adopt a policy. The adoption does nothing." Action, by contrast, "scares everyone, not just the actor."

## Unenforced Speech Codes Are Still Powerful

Yet the very adoption of hate speech policies has influenced behavior on several campuses. This point was repeated to me by many administrators at the schools I visited, who reported the rise of a "culture of civility" that eschews, if not informally sanctions, hateful speech. "Don't mistake symbolism for impotence," they regularly reminded me. Symbols shape and reflect social meaning, providing cues to the community about the range of acceptable behavior. Adopting a hate speech policy, then, could have persuasive power even if it were rarely enforced. Consider the dean of students at a northeastern liberal arts college, who spoke proudly of her school's hate speech policy. Had the policy been formally invoked, I asked. "Rarely," she told me, but the measure "sets a standard on campus. It gives us something we can point our finger to in the catalog to remind students of the expectations and rights we all have in the community." This sentiment was repeated by the president of a well-known institution, who claimed that "we didn't set out to enforce the policy punitively but to use it as the basis for our educational efforts at respecting individuality." Still another administrator admitted that, "while we've rarely used the policy formally, it does give support to students who believe their rights have been violated. They'll come in for informal mediation and point to the policy as the reason for why the other person must stop harassing them."

Sociologists would call this process norm production— that symbolic measures can condition and order behavior without the actual implementation of punitive mechanisms. Hate speech policies set an expected standard of behavior on campus; college officials employ orientation sessions, extracurricular programs, and campus dialogue to inculcate and spread the message; and over time an expectation begins to take root that hate speech is unacceptable and should be prohibited. Of course, this mechanism makes regulation a self-policing exercise—colleges need not take formal or punitive action—but the effect is to perpetuate a collective norm that sees hate speech as undesirable and worthy of prohibition. Moreover, considering the isomorphic tendencies of college administrators, the creation of speech policies—or speech norms—at respected and prestigious institutions has a "trickle down" effect throughout academe. Again, sociologists would call this process normative isomorphism, but most people know the phenomenon as "keeping up with the Joneses." If Harvard, Berkeley, or Brown passes measures against hate speech, then institutions lower in the academic food chain are likely to take note and follow suit. If prestigious institutions advance campus norms that eschew hate speech, then both peer and "wannabe" institutions are likely to consider and replicate such informal rules. Indeed, this is the very fear of FIRE and its compatriots—that if PC [politically correct] policies are not checked now, their message will spread throughout academe infecting other campuses. What FIRE fails to say, but undoubtedly must be thinking, is that informal law and mass constitutionalism are at stake if the spread of speech regulation is not curbed. FIRE can hang its hat on *R.A.V.* [*v. City of St. Paul*], *Doe* [*v. University of Michigan*], *UWM Post* [*v. Board of Regents of the University of Wisconsin*], and the other court cases in which judges have overturned college hate speech policies, but as hate speech regulation continues to flourish on college campuses, informal speech norms are at stake throughout the larger bounds of civil society.

## Student Support of Speech Codes

Whatever one thinks of FIRE and its agenda, its supporters are like the old-fashioned fire brigade that excitedly shows up at a burning building only to toss paltry pails of water on the inferno. Hate speech regulation has already crossed the fire-break between academe and the rest of civil society and is well on its way toward acceptance in other influential institutions. The initial signs are found in surveys of incoming college freshmen. Shortly after *R.A.V.*, researchers began asking new freshmen whether they believe that "colleges should prohibit racist/sexist speech on campus." In a 1993 survey, 58 percent of first-year students supported hate speech regulation, a number that has stayed steady and even grown a bit in the years following. By 1994, two-thirds of incoming freshmen approved of hate speech prohibitions, with more recent results leveling off around 60 percent. Unfortunately, there are not similar surveys before 1993 to compare these results against, but it is a safe bet that support would have been minimal through the mid-1980s when the issue had not yet achieved salience. More to the point, the surveys show that support for speech regulation is achieved *before* students ever set foot on campus. If, as the codes' opponents claim, colleges are indoctrinating students in favor of speech regulation, the influence has reached beyond campus borders. New students are being socialized to this norm in society even before they attend college.

---

*Surveys of the general population show an increasing queasiness with hate speech and a greater willingness to regulate such expression.*

---

## General Public Supports Speech Codes

So too, surveys of the general population show an increasing queasiness with hate speech and a greater willingness to regulate such expression privately, especially when communicated over the Internet. In 1991, at the height of the speech code controversy, the CBS News/New York Times Poll asked the following question of American adults:

Some universities have adopted codes of conduct under which students may be expelled for using derogatory language with respect to blacks, Jews, women, homosexuals and other groups of students. Which of the following comes closest to your view about this?

A. Students who insult other students in this fashion should be subject to punishment; or

B. The Bill of Rights protects free speech for these students, and they should not be subject to punishment.

Among respondents, 60 percent agreed that hate speech deserved punishment; only 32 percent believed that the Bill of Rights should protect such expression, with 8 percent undecided.

In 1994 the National Opinion Research Center (NORC) took the issue beyond campuses, asking a national sample whether, "under the First Amendment guaranteeing free speech, people should be allowed to express their own opinions even if they are harmful or offensive to members of other religious or racial groups." At the time, 63 percent of respondents agreed, although only 21 percent did so strongly. However, when NORC dropped a direct reference to the First Amendment, asking whether "people should not be allowed to express opinions that are harmful or offensive to members of other religious or racial groups," respondents were split almost evenly in their opinions. Forty-one percent supported such restrictions, 44 percent opposed them, and the remainder were either neutral or unsure.

Both the CBS News/New York Times and NORC surveys were conducted in the early 1990s, as the speech code controversy was being played out on the front pages of major media. If respondents at the time seemed comfortable with different rules for separate venues—approving of hate speech measures on campus but split over regulations in larger society—this divergence seemed to narrow by the end of the decade. In

1999 the Freedom Forum conducted a State of the First Amendment Survey. Among its several questions, the Forum queried:

> I am now going to read you some ways that people might exercise their First Amendment right of free speech. . . . [Do you believe that] people should be allowed to use words in public that might be offensive to racial groups?

Even with the explicit reference to the First Amendment and the right of free speech, researchers found that 78 percent of respondents disagreed with the exhortation to open discourse. Indeed, an amazing 61 percent of respondents strongly disagreed with the statement, indicating a presumed willingness to regulate or restrict racial hate speech. The Freedom Forum has repeated this survey annually, and although support for hate speech regulation has dropped a bit, the level still hovers around two-thirds assent.

---

*There seems to be a burgeoning sense that hate speech, and particularly racist speech, warrants proscription.*

---

## Hate Speech Online

The results from the Freedom Forum's surveys are in line with other polling data about hate speech involving computers and the Internet. In 1999, National Public Radio, the Kaiser Foundation, and Harvard's Kennedy School of Government teamed up to query Americans' attitudes about government. As part of that survey, researchers asked two questions about online hate speech. Finding that over 80 percent of respondents believed that hate speech on the Internet was a problem, the survey asked whether "the government should do something about" these attacks against a person's "race, religion, or ethnicity." Nearly two-thirds of respondents believed the problem required governmental action, a number consistent with the 60 percent of respondents in a study by Princeton Survey Research Associates who agreed that "the government should put major new restrictions on the Internet to limit access to pornography, hate speech, and information about bomb-making or other crimes."

We should be careful not to overstate these results. The surveys do *not* show that Americans have become less supportive of the First Amendment, for other polling reflects continued attachment to open discourse and free speech. Moreover, many of these surveys are limited to a specific mode of hate speech—expression over the Internet. For that matter, the Freedom Forum's surveys consistently show that respondents oppose a formal law prohibiting hate speech, presumably preferring that regulation be handled informally. Yet there has been a significant change afoot, a sizeable shift in popular norms of free speech as the line dividing valuable speech from harmful expression has been moved. Open discourse is still important, respondents appear to say, but just as fighting words may be restricted, there seems to be a burgeoning sense that hate speech, and particularly racist speech, warrants proscription.

# Schools Must Not Use American Indian Mascots, Logos, and Nicknames

*Cornel D. Pewewardy*

*Cornel D. Pewewardy is an associate professor in the Department of Teaching and Leadership at the University of Kansas in Lawrence.*

Every school year, classroom teachers face the reality and challenge of educating diverse children in a multicultural society. Teaching multiculturally requires educators to examine sensitive, diverse topics and cultural issues. It means looking at historical and contemporary events from various perspectives, rather than a single one. Teachers and administrators whose knowledge of history and current events is monocultural in scope and who are unaware of their own prejudices are likely to hinder the academic success and personal development of many students, however unintentional this may be. Multicultural teaching encourages students to investigate the institutional racism, classism, and sexism that have served different populations in discriminatory ways. Educators can help monocultural classes and schools examine their own biases and stereotypes related to different cultural groups. Although one's ethnic group is just one of a number of possible identity sources, ethnicity is at the heart of the equity problem in American society. Therefore, discussions about achieving educational excellence should address those ethnic groups that have been consistently cut off from equal access to a quality education.

Cornel D. Pewewardy, "Playing Indian at Halftime: The Controversy over American Indian Mascots, Logos, and Nicknames in School-Related Events," *The Clearing House*, vol. 77, no. 5, May/June 2004, pp. 180–84. Copyright © 2004 by Helen Dwight Reid Educational Foundation. Reproduced with permission of the Helen Dwight Reid Educational Foundation. Published by Heldref Publications, 1319 18th St., NW, Washington, DC, 20036-1802.

Educators have a professional responsibility to eliminate racism in all aspects of school life. Accordingly, educators should not ignore multicultural issues in school. Instead, these issues should become teachable moments in which these concerns are confronted and discussed. Accurate information can begin to displace the myths that many students hold about others. Today, one teachable moment is the controversy over using American Indian mascots, logos, and nicknames in school-related events. Supporters of such mascots claim they honor American Indian people, embody institutional traditions, foster a shared identity, and intensify the pleasures of sports and athletics. According to those who oppose them, however, the mascots give life to racial stereotypes, as well as revivify historical patterns of appropriation and oppression. These results often foster discomfort and pain among American Indian people.

Non-Indian people may not be culturally aware that some American Indian symbols used by cheerleaders and cheering fans—war chants, peace pipes, eagle feathers, war bonnets, and dances—are highly revered or even sacred in many American Indian tribal communities. Many mascots, logos, and nicknames represent stereotypical and racist images that relegate American Indian people to a colonial representation of history. The exploitation of Indian mascots, logos, and nicknames in schools is, in reality, an issue of decolonization and educational equity. . . .

## Countering the Assault of Native American Nicknames

Using the word *countering*, which means to confront defensive or retaliatory attacks or arguments, to describe certain behaviors and thinking in our society is a strong indictment of the existing social fabric of the United States. Many educators in this country are serious players when it comes to countering racism, thereby protecting the mental health of school children today. However, many more teachers are unresponsive to or unaware of the issues of racism in schools today. Like these teachers, parents, educators, and liberals who deny being racists but remain silent when confronted with the issue also allow institutional racism to continue.

This issue has turned into a debate and torn schools and communities apart. Administrators spend months fending off angry alumni on both sides of the issue, calming students, and dealing with mainstream news media that oversimplify these issues. After it is all over, school districts often must spend additional time and energy healing the wounds and community ruptures left in the wake of efforts to counter institutional racism by eradicating American Indian mascots, logos, and nicknames in schools.

## "Playing Indian" Is Racist

Many schools around the country "play Indian" by exhibiting American Indian mascots, logos, and nicknames at sporting events: school bands play so-called "Indian" fight songs (for example, "One-little-two-little-three-little Indians . . .") during both pregame and halftime entertainment; mascots dress in stereotypical cartoon character-like costumes and beat hand drums and/or carry foam tomahawks; and fans do the "tomahawk chop" in unison. These all are inauthentic representations of American Indian cultures. Many school officials claim they are honoring American Indians and insist that the activities are not offensive. I argue otherwise and contend that these racist activities are forms of cultural violence in schools.

After studying this issue for fifteen years, I found that groups outside the American Indian community imposed most Indian mascots, logos, and nicknames on athletic teams. Even in the earliest U.S. government boarding schools, Indian children had no involvement in choosing their schools' mascots, logos, and nicknames. For example, the first recorded instance of an "Indian" nickname for a sports team was in 1894 at the Carlisle Indian School, an off-reservation U.S. government boarding school for American Indian students, located in Carlisle, Pennsylvania. Mainstream sports journalists praised the team's football performance in the early years of their program. From 1894 until 1917, the Carlisle football team defeated the major power football team of the day. Subsequently, opposing college football teams and sports media nicknamed team members the Carlisle "Indians." Ironically, most American Indians have always opposed the use of "Indian" mascots, logos, and nicknames for sports teams. Yet, these traditions of doing so are enthusiastically supported by most European Americans.

Although images of Indians in mainstream sports culture have become as American as apple pie and baseball, educators should be aware that American Indians never would have associated sacred practices with the hoopla of high school pep rallies and halftime entertainments.

---

*Many European Americans rely on these manufactured images [of Indians] to anchor them to the land and verify a false account of a shared history.*

---

## Indian Mascots Are Demeaning

The unfortunate portrayal of Indian mascots in sports today takes many forms. Some teams use generic Indian names—such as Indians, Braves, Warriors, or Chiefs—while others adopt specific tribal names—such as Seminoles, Comanches, or Apaches. Indian mascots exhibit either idealized or comical facial features and native dress, ranging from body-length feathered (usually turkey) headdresses to fake buckskin attire or skimpy loincloths. Some teams and supporters display counterfeit Indian paraphernalia, including foam tomahawks, feathers, face paints, drums, and pipes. They also use mock "Indian" behaviors, such as the tomahawk chop, dances, war chants (for example, at Florida State University), drum beating, war-whooping, and symbolic scalping. Many European Americans rely on these manufactured images to anchor them to the land and verify a false account of a shared history. These "Indians," however, exist only in the imagination: they provide a self-serving historical connection that leaves actual American Indian people untethered and rootless in or erased from the historical accounts of European Americans.

Many school officials are all too familiar with the current legal and educational battles toward eliminating Indian mascots, logos, and nicknames from school-related events. The U.S. Commission on Civil Rights (CCR), the highest official governmental body of its kind, issued a strong statement in 2001 condemning their use and recommending that schools eliminate Indian images and nicknames as sports symbols (U.S. Department of Justice 2001). Grassroots efforts of thousands of American Indian parents nationwide prompted this decision among CCR members. Moreover, the critical mass of American Indian educational organizations and professionals supported the CCR statement. American Indian educators showed school officials that negative images, symbols, and behaviors play a crucial role in distorting and warping American Indian children's cultural perceptions of themselves, as well as non-Indian children's attitudes toward and simplistic understanding of American Indian culture. Hollywood scriptwriters originally manufactured most of these stereotypes. Over time, they have evolved into contemporary racist images that prevent millions of school-age students from understanding American Indians' past and present experiences.

## Impact on Children's Self-Esteem

Children begin to develop racial awareness at an early age, perhaps as early as three or four years old. Clinical psychologists have established that negative stereotypes and derogatory images engender and perpetuate undemocratic and unhealthy attitudes in children, plaguing them for years to come. Many non-Indian children exposed to these Hollywood stereotypes at early ages grow into adults who may unwittingly or unknowingly discriminate against American Indians. These children have been prevented from developing authentic, healthy attitudes about Indians. Moreover, Indian children who constantly see themselves being stereotyped and their cultures belittled grow into adults who feel and act inferior to other people. These racial and inauthentic behaviors mock Indian culture and cause many Indian youngsters to have low self-esteem and feel shame about their cultural identity. School environments should be places where students unlearn negative stereotypes that such mascots represent and promote. However, athletic events where Indian mascots are frequently used teach children the exact opposite.

Perhaps some people at these sporting events do not hear the foul language being shouted out in the stands and seating arenas associated with the usage of Indian mascots, logos, and nicknames. The most obvious offenses are the terms *redskins* (lady redskins) and *squaws*. According to one explanation, the word *redskin* originated in early colonial times when European colonists paid bounties for Indians' red skins—thereby coining the term *redskin*. The word *squaw* is a French corruption of the Iroquois word *otsiskwa*, meaning female properties. Both words are almost always used in a derogatory fashion in sporting events. Although these terms may be facing increasing social disdain, they certainly are far from dead. These words accentuate the differences in appearance, culture, gender, nationality, or sexual orientation of people and underplay—if not to deny—the similarities between people.

Given this background, no one, especially those associated with schools, should allow students to adopt a cartoon version of American Indian cultures as a mascot or logo. Educators and students need to be more educated about the negative effects of racist Indian mascots and logos on American Indian people. Many students do not recognize that the Indian mascot issue is as important in the American Indian community as alcoholism, substance abuse, and poverty. Some people excuse their ambivalence on the issue by saying there is "too much fuss over team names," "we're just having fun," "we're not harming anybody," or "what's the point?" They miss the connection because they are removed from the issues of American Indian education. It is hard to take American Indians seriously or to empathize with them when they are always portrayed as speaking in old, broken, stoic Indian clichés, such as "many moons ago"; dressed up in Halloween or Thanksgiving costumes; or acting crazy like a "bunch of wild Indians." These make-believe Indians are prohibited from changing over time to be like real people. On athletic fields and in gymnasiums, they are denied the dignity of their tribal histories, the validity of their major contributions to modern American society, and the distinctiveness of their multitribal identities. . . .

## Racist Images of American Indians

Despite years of cultural diversity teacher training and integration of multicultural education lesson plans into the school curricula, children still play "cowboys and Indians" at some schools. Most teachers, undoubtedly, have seen (or perhaps even supported) children running around in turkey feathers and cardboard headbands, carrying homemade bows and arrows, patting a hand against their mouth and yelling "woo-woo-woo," or raising their hands over their shoulder and saying "how." The perpetuation of these invented Indian behaviors reflects the influence of peer socialization, schooling, and mainstream movies. They mock American Indian cultural practices, demean actual human beings, and treat American Indian people as subhumans incapable of verbal communication. This manufactured image of the Indian as something wild and inferior implies white superiority, a value judgment made namely by Hollywood scriptwriters.

Another popular character born of the racist images of American Indian people is the clown. Traditional clown societies of many tribes (for example, Apaches, Pueblos) attempt to make their people laugh during celebrations and ceremonies. On the other hand, the contemporary clown, born of American popular culture is more like the jester or the fool, the inferior one responsible for making his superiors laugh. The use of clowns has always been a major way to assert dominance over a particular person or a certain group of people. During ballgames, the exaggerated images of Indians become clown-like, serving to manipulate and keep in place negative images during school-related events.

However, I hypothesize that the use of American Indian mascots in sporting events was influenced by the philosophical views of the Enlightenment and the developing Romantic movement. During those periods, American Indians were seen either as amusing exotics or as Noble Savages, excellent types for representing ideas in literature, in film, or on the stage. But the reality was that these figures were never more than white characters with cliché comic or noble personalities, thinly disguised in red skins and feathered costumes. American Indian people were never considered real human beings whose existence might be dramatically interesting.

## Education Is an Answer to Racism

Who should decide what is demeaning and racist? Clearly, the affected party determines what is offensive. Unaffected members of society should not dictate how the affected party should feel. Moreover, efforts to retire Indian mascots, logos, and nicknames should not be met with ugly alumni and student backlashes that label grassroots complainants as troublemakers, activist, militant, gadflies, or practitioners of political correctness. Therefore, educators who advocate and affirm cultural diversity must be ready for a challenge. Only a concerted effort to debunk Hollywood's mythology can alter the distorted image of the American Indian people for the better.

Educators should examine the biases and stereotypes their students hold. These stereotypes, caused by ignorance, hard times, and folk wisdom socialization, can be countered by accurate and culturally responsive information. Education can become a tool for liberation from bigotry—rather than a facilitator of racism. . . .

## A Challenge to Teachers

The ongoing use of Indian mascots in school-sponsored events is an issue of educational equity. Therefore, my professional challenge is to educators. As long as such mascots remain within the arena of school activities, both Indian and non-Indian children are learning to tolerate racism in schools. By tolerating the use of demeaning stereotypes in our public schools, we further desensitize entire generations of children. As a result, schools reinforce the stereotypical negative images projected in the broader mainstream American cultural imagination. Sports teams with Indian mascots, logos, and nicknames teach them that it is acceptable to demean a race or group of people through American sports culture. Educators must turn the use of these mascots, logos, and nicknames into powerful teaching moments that could help counter the fabricated images and manufactured pictures of Indians that most school-age children have ingrained in their psyche by one hundred years of mass media. Finally, I challenge administrators and policymakers to provide the intellectual school leadership that truly embraces multicultural education, helping to eliminate the cultural violence associated with and triggered by the use of American Indian mascots in school-related events.

# Europe Must Ban Internet Hate Speech

*Michel Barnier*

*Michel Barnier is France's minister for foreign affairs.*

I wanted to open this special meeting of the OSCE [Organization for Security and Co-operation in Europe] for many reasons, because of the quality of the delegations present here and because the stakes are high. Every person of my generation has at some time or other had a dream, the same dream— that of the great African humanist, Léopold Sedar Senghor, who said: "I dreamed of a world flooded with sunshine in fraternity with my blue-eyed brothers".

And yet this dream is rather far from being realized. The struggle is not at an end. Injustice and intolerance continue to strike, all about us and sometimes in our own homes.

Why conceal the truth? I am a citizen of a country which has just experienced, since 1 January this year [2004], an unprecedented number of anti-Semitic acts. But I am also a minister of a government which is fighting to prevent, identify, sanction and combat such acts.

France wanted to host this special meeting of the OSCE, and I want to thank the Chairman-in-Office, the Bulgarian Minister for Foreign Affairs, Mr. Solomon Passy, the Secretary General of the Organization, the delegates representing your 55 participating States as well as six partner States, the civil society representatives, the Internet professionals and each and every one of you, men and women alike, for having accepted the invitation to attend.

Michel Barnier, "Statement at the OSCE (Organization for Security and Co-operation in Europe) Meeting on the Relationship Between Racist, Xenophobic and Anti-Semitic Propaganda on the Internet and Hate Crimes," osce.org, June 16, 2004. Reproduced by permission.

## This Is a Critical Time for Europe

This is a critical time for us, a key stage in our common struggle against intolerance, following the very important work done at the conference last April in Berlin [Germany] on anti-Semitism, and preceding the Brussels [Belgium] conference in September this year which is to be devoted to racism and xenophobia.

I should like to mention to you three convictions which prompt France's struggle against intolerance. The first conviction of France is that we must say, among ourselves and to all about us, what is the truth on this subject. It must not be disguised, minimized or treated as something commonplace.

In fact the truth is that, while intolerance may not have won the day, it has made progress almost everywhere in Europe during these last few years, relying in particular on an instrument which is at once new and extraordinary, namely the Internet. We naturally do not want to question in any way the existence of the Internet. We are all aware, moreover, of the exceptional contribution the Internet is making to the spread of knowledge, the understanding of identities and dialogue among people.

---

*The Internet has been taken hostage by the networks of intolerance and it requires a fully appropriate response.*

---

## Intolerance Has Taken the Internet Hostage

But it is our duty to stress that by virtue of its characteristics—immediacy and anonymity in particular—the Internet has had a seductive influence on networks of intolerance. It has placed at their disposal its formidable power of amplification, diffusion and connection. A study recently carried out in the United Kingdom and bearing on 15 participating States of the OSCE shows that in the course of four years, from 2000 to 2004, the number of violent and extremist sites has increased by 300 per cent. This means that the Internet has been taken hostage by the networks of intolerance and it requires a fully appropriate response from us.

Our second conviction is that we must take account of the harmfulness of acts of intolerance in their full scope; in other words, the full reality that they represent. In France we feel that there must be a clear relationship, as is in fact indicated by the title of our meeting, between racist, anti-Semitic or xenophobic propaganda on the one hand and hate crimes on the other. That is why we are not here only to condemn insults or abject statements. We are here to fight against statements which, once uttered and sometimes repeated, may lead to crime; for this is the reality that we find, alas, in many cases.

## Free Speech Is Not Unlimited

What is at issue for us is not freedom of speech but appeals or incitement to commit particular acts. When an insult leads to crime it changes its nature; it becomes a veritable act of intellectual premeditation. I may observe in passing that our various nations guarantee freedom of speech, but without leaving it completely unlimited, on the understanding that such limits as are set must be clearly defined by law.

The third and final conviction that I want to express here, in the name of France, is that a single response will not be adequate in combating the new methods and the new paths of intolerance.

A response involving prevention is indispensable but not in itself adequate. It is not without its weaknesses. Acts of intolerance are on the increase. We must be capable of acting directly against them and, when required, against those who commit them. It is important then to seek an appropriate balance between prevention and action.

Who is to do this?

Each one of us, in the first instance, within the sphere of his own responsibility, wherever he may be, and above all within the national framework. This is the objective that has been pursued by the French Government during the last two years under the aegis of the President of the Republic and the Prime Minister. We sized up what was going on in our country and responded, among other things, by making the sanctions applicable to racially-motivated crime, anti-Semitism and xenophobia more severe; by stressing the responsibility of website hosts; by focusing on a precise and systematic search for expressions of intolerance in the media—in sum, then, by providing methods and tools for exercising vigilance and constant surveillance, but also by seeking opportunities for dialogue with the industry and for applying sanctions to the authors of these crimes.

## Europe Must Unite Against Intolerance

At the same time, since the French response is active and, as I believe, recognized as being so, I am in a good position to gauge the limits imposed on the actions of any single nation. The Internet has no frontiers. We need instruments. Some of these exist, and they are useful. France has signed the United Nations Convention on the Elimination of All Forms of Racial Discrimination. It has also signed the Council of Europe's Convention on Cybercrime together with its additional protocol.

By taking into consideration the growth of intolerance and giving thought to methods of curbing it, the OSCE is playing a role perfectly suited to it, particularly within the context of its mission to strengthen collective security. Thanks in particular to the work done in Berlin, to which our Secretary of State for Foreign Affairs, Mr. Renaud Muselier, made a valuable contribution, and thanks also to the work being done in Paris today and to be done in Brussels tomorrow, the OSCE can help us to see the situation more clearly both as regards our objectives and the means most appropriate for combating intolerance on the Internet. As for the objectives, we must establish collectively a realistic level of ambition but a level which enables us to cope with statements marked by intolerance and the acts which they inspire. I have already expressed the wish that France should go well beyond simple prevention.

---

*We must . . . propose to our citizens not only an analysis of intolerance but also concrete, active and operational responses which will curb intolerance.*

---

## The OSCE Must Draft an Internet Code of Conduct

As for the means, the OSCE must become their observatory, or let's say their laboratory. As for the role of the observatory, it is essential to identify good practices and to improve our understanding of their value and means of operation. As for the laboratory role, the OSCE must, relying on the available expertise, consider the matter thoroughly and formulate proposals which might in the end lead to the drafting of, for example, a code of conduct.

However, at this stage let us concentrate less on instruments than on procedures. It is essential, if we wish to attain our goals, that our procedures should be truly rooted in partnership, bringing together States, non-governmental organizations, and those who can provide the access required.

The state of urgency created by the rise of intolerance, the scope of the work to be accomplished, all these things are bound to make the OSCE's Ministerial Council in Sofia [Bulgaria] during the autumn a moment of truth. We must be in a position to propose to our citizens not only an analysis of intolerance but also concrete, active and operational responses which will curb intolerance. In keeping with its traditional values, France would like to emphasize the effectiveness of a response in keeping with the law and based on the collective efforts of nations. We must succeed, because for our societies intolerance is intolerable in whatever form it may appear— racism, xenophobia or anti-Semitism. These are three distinct forms of intolerance, but they must be fought together. This is a great challenge to which the OSCE has resolved to address itself; but at the same time it is a splendid opportunity for the Organization and for an effective display of multilaterism in general.

# Campus Hate Speech Codes Should Be Eliminated

*Harvey Silverglate and Greg Lukianoff*

*Harvey Silverglate is a cofounder of the Foundation for Individual Rights in Education (FIRE). The foundation is dedicated to preserving and enlarging academic freedom, due process, freedom of speech, and freedom of conscience on American college campuses. Greg Lukianoff is a First Amendment attorney and coauthor of FIRE's* Guide to Free Speech on Campus.

[In 1998], a higher-education editor for *The New York Times* informed one of us, Harvey Silverglate, that Neil L. Rudenstine—then president of Harvard University—had insisted that Harvard did not have, much less enforce, any "speech codes." Silverglate suggested the editor dig deeper, because virtually any undergraduate could contest the president's claim.

A mere three years earlier, the faculty of the Harvard Law School had adopted "Sexual Harassment Guidelines" targeted at "seriously offensive" speech. The guidelines were passed in response to a heated campus controversy involving a law-student parody of an expletive-filled *Harvard Law Review* article that promoted a postmodernist, gender-related view of the nature of law. In response to an outcry by outraged campus feminists and their allies, a law professor lodged a formal complaint against the parodists with the college's administrative board.

When the board dismissed the charge on the technicality that the law school had no speech code that would specifically outlaw such a parody, the dean at the time appointed a faculty committee to draft the guidelines, which remain in force to-

Harvey Silverglate and Greg Lukianoff, "Speech Codes: Alive and Well on Campus," *Chronicle of Higher Education*, vol. 49, no. 47, August 1, 2003, p. B7. Reproduced by permission of the authors.

day. The intention was to prevent, or punish if necessary, future offensive gender-related speech that might create a "hostile environment" for female law students at Harvard. As far as Silverglate (who lives and works near the Harvard campus and follows events there closely) has observed, there has not been a truly biting parody on hot-button issues related to gender politics at the law school since.

[In the fall of 2002], officials at Harvard Business School admonished and threatened with punishment an editor of the school's student-run newspaper for publishing a cartoon critical of the administration. He resigned in protest over the administration's assault on the paper's editorial independence.

---

*The Foundation for Individual Rights in Education defines a speech code as* any campus regulation that punishes, forbids, heavily regulates, or restricts a substantial amount of protected speech.

---

At virtually the same time, after a controversy in which a law student was accused of racially insensitive speech, a cry went up for adopting "Discriminatory Harassment Guidelines" to parallel the code that outlawed gender-based insults. As the controversy progressed, some students accused two professors of insensitivity for trying to discuss the issues in class. Soon after the Black Law Students Association demanded that one of those professors be disciplined and banned from teaching required first-year classes, he announced that he would not teach his course for the rest of the semester. The other professor insisted on continuing to teach, but the dean's office announced that all of his classes had to be tape-recorded so that any students who felt offended being in his presence could instead listen to the recorded lecture.

All of that at a university that, as President Rudenstine supposedly assured *The New York Times*, did not have, much less enforce, a speech code.

## Speech Codes Are Alive and Well

Today, many in higher education still share Rudenstine's apparent belief that a speech code exists only if it is prominently stamped SPEECH CODE in the student handbook. To them, any speech code is an anachronism, a failed relic of the 1980s that has disappeared from all but the most repressive backwaters of academe.

But speech codes are alive and well, if one is realistic about what makes a campus regulation a speech code. The Foundation for Individual Rights in Education defines a speech code as *any campus regulation that punishes, forbids, heavily regulates, or restricts a substantial amount of protected speech.* Thus defined, speech codes are the rule rather than the exception in higher education.

Why does virtually no college call its speech code by that name? For one thing, in the 1980s and '90s, every legal challenge of a clearly identified speech code at a public institution was successful. To maintain a weapon against speech that is "offensive" or "uncivil" (or merely too robust), the authors of the current stealthier generation of speech codes have adopted highly restrictive "speech zone" policies, e-mail policies that ban "offensive" speech, "diversity statements" with provisions that punish those uttering any "intolerant expression," and, of course, the ubiquitous "harassment policies" aimed at "hostile" viewpoints and words that operate by redefining speech as a form of conduct.

## FIRE Wants to End Codes

FIRE initiated, in April [2003], a litigation project aimed at abolishing such codes at public colleges and universities, beginning with a lawsuit charging that various policies at Shippensburg University are unconstitutional. Shippensburg promises only to protect speech that does not "provoke, harass, demean, intimidate, or harm another." Shippensburg's "Racism and Cultural Diversity" statement (modified by the uni-

versity after FIRE filed suit) defined harassment as "unsolic-
ited, unwanted conduct which annoys, threatens, or alarms a
person or group." Shippensburg also has "speech zones" that
restrict protests to only two areas on the campus.

In a recent *Chronicle [of Higher Education]* article,
Shippensburg's president, Anthony F. Ceddia, complained that
FIRE had "cobbled together words and expressions of different
policies and procedures." That is true; it found unconstitutional provisions in many different places—the student handbook and the university's Web site, to cite just two—and is
challenging all of them.

---

*There is no excuse for a liberal-arts institution, public or
private, to punish speech, no matter how impolite, impolitic, unpopular, or ornery.*

---

FIRE has been developing an online database of policies
that restrict speech on both private and public campuses.
Given the longstanding assumption that academic freedom at
liberal-arts colleges protects offensive and unpopular speech,
the number and variety of such policies are startling. FIRE's
still-in-progress survey and analysis demonstrates that a clear
majority of higher-education institutions have substantial
speech restrictions and many others have lesser restrictions
that still, arguably, infringe on academic freedom.

## Colleges Limit Free Speech

Some codes, of course, are worse than others. Some are pa-
tently unconstitutional; others, artfully written by offices of
general counsels, seek to obfuscate their intention to prohibit
or discourage certain speech. However, there is no excuse for a
liberal-arts institution, public or private, to punish speech, no
matter how impolite, impolitic, unpopular, or ornery.

No one denies that a college can and should ban true harassment—but a code that *calls* itself a "racial-harassment

code" does not thereby magically inoculate itself against free-speech and academic-freedom obligations. The recent controversy over "racial harassment" at Harvard Law School has been replicated on campuses across the country, often with outcomes as perilous to academic freedom. For example, in 1999, a professor at the Columbia University School of Law administered a criminal-law exam posing a complex question concerning the issues of feticide, abortion, violence against women, and consent to violence. Some women in the class complained to two faculty members, who then told the law-school dean that the professor's exam was so insensitive to the women in the class that it may have constituted harassment. The dean brought the case to Columbia's general counsel before concluding—correctly of course—after a dialogue with FIRE that academic freedom absolutely protected the professor.

---

*It should be obvious that allowing colleges to promulgate broad and amorphous rules that can punish speech, regardless of the intention, will result in self-censoring and administrative abuses.*

---

Such examples demonstrate the persistence of the notion that administrators may muzzle speech that some students find "offensive," in the name of protecting civil rights. Further, the continuing existence of these codes relies on people's unwillingness to criticize any restriction that sports the "progressive" veneer of preventing racial or sexual "harassment"—even when the codes themselves go far beyond the traditional boundaries of academic and constitutional freedom. Fortunately, some see these codes for what they are and recognize that there is nothing progressive about censorship.

## Speech Codes Result in Abuses

It should be obvious that allowing colleges to promulgate broad and amorphous rules that can punish speech, regardless of the intention, will result in self-censoring and administrative abuses. Consider the case of Mercedes Lynn de Uriarte, a professor at the University of Texas at Austin. In 1999, after filing an employment grievance, she received notice that the campus's office of equal employment opportunity [EEO] had chosen to investigate her for "ethnic harassment" of another professor in her department. Both de Uriarte and the accusing professor were Mexican-American. The facts suggest that the ethnic-harassment accusation was little more than an excuse for the university to retaliate against de Uriarte for filing the grievance. After nine months of pressing de Uriarte to answer personal questions about her beliefs and why she disliked the other professor, the EEO office concluded that there was no evidence of "ethnic harassment" but scolded de Uriarte for "harboring personal animosity" toward the other professor and for not being sufficiently cooperative with the investigating dean.

In 2001 at Tufts University, a female undergraduate filed sexual-harassment charges against a student publication, citing a sexual-harassment code and claiming a satirical cartoon and text made her a "sex object." A vocal member of the Student Labor Action Movement [SLAM], she was offended when the paper mocked "oh-so-tight" SLAM tank tops (amid other jokes about Madonna and President Bush). Hearings were initiated. FIRE successfully persuaded the hearing panel to reject the attempted censorship.

Those are just two examples among dozens that FIRE has seen where speech codes are used against students or faculty members. They illustrate not only that these codes are enforced, but that they are enforced against speech that would be clearly protected in the larger society.

## Speech Codes Used to Silence Mild Expressions

Moreover, virtually none of the cases that FIRE has dealt with have followed the paradigm that "hate-speech codes" were supposedly crafted to combat: the intentional hurling of an epithet at a member of a racial or sexual minority. Overwhelmingly, speech codes are used against much milder expression, or even against expression of a particular unpopular or officially disfavored viewpoint.

The situation of Steve Hinkle, a student at California Polytechnic State University, is another case in point. In the fall of 2002, he posted fliers for a speech by C. Mason Weaver, the author of *It's OK to Leave the Plantation*. In his book, Weaver, an African-American writer, argues that government-assistance programs place many black people in a cycle of poverty and dependence similar to slavery. The flier included the place and time of the speech, the name of the book, and the author's picture. When Hinkle tried to post a flier in one public area, several students approached him and demanded that he not post the "offensive" flier. One student actually called the campus police, whose reports note that the students complained of "a suspicious white male passing out literature of an offensive racial nature." Hinkle was subjected to administrative hearings over the next half year and was found guilty of "disruption" for trying to post the flier.

Unless one considers posting a flier with factually accurate information a "hate crime," it is clear such speech codes are used to punish speech that administrators or students simply dislike. That should not come as a surprise to any student of history. When broad powers and unchecked authority are granted to officials—even for what are claimed to be the noblest of goals—those powers will be abused. Indeed, the Supreme Court has ruled unequivocally that "hate-speech laws," in contrast to "hate-crimes laws," are unconstitutional. Yet most of the speech prosecuted on college campuses does not even rise to the level of hate speech.

Some argue that speech codes communicate to students the kind of society to which we all *should* aspire. That is perhaps the most pernicious of all justifications, for it makes unexamined assumptions about the power of administrators to reach intrusively into the hearts and consciences of students. There is nothing ideal about a campus where protests and leaflets are quarantined to tiny, remote "speech zones," or where being inoffensive is a higher value than intellectual engagement.

Yet even if one agrees with such "aspirations," it is antithetical to a liberal-arts college to coerce others into sharing them. The threat of sanctions crosses the clear line between *encouraging* such aspirations and *coercing* fealty to them, whether genuine or affected. An administrator's employing the suasion of the bully pulpit differs crucially from using authority to bully disfavored opinions into submission.

---

*In the long run, speech codes—actively enforced or not— send the message that it is OK to ban controversial or arguably ugly expressions that some do not wish to hear.*

---

## Speech Codes Are Chilling

Some people contend that the codes are infrequently enforced. The facts demonstrate otherwise, but even if a campus never enforced its speech code, the code would remain a palpable form of coercion. As long as the policy exists, the *threat* of enforcement remains real and will inevitably influence some people's speech. In First Amendment law, that is known as a "chilling" effect: Merely by disseminating the codes in student handbooks, administrators can prevent much of the speech they disfavor. Students, seeing what is banned—or even guessing at what might be banned as they struggle with the breadth or vagueness of the definitions—will play it safe and avoid engaging in speech that, even though constitutionally protected, may offend a student or a disciplinary board.

In the long run, speech codes—actively enforced or not— send the message that it is OK to ban controversial or arguably ugly expressions that some do not wish to hear. Students will not forget that lesson once they get their diplomas. A whole generation of American students is learning that its members should hide their deeply held unpopular beliefs, while other students realize that they have the power, even the right, to censor opinions they dislike.

Take the case at Ithaca College [in the spring of 2003], when the College Republicans brought to campus Bay Buchanan, the sister of Patrick Buchanan, for a speech entitled "The Failures of Feminism." Instead of protesting the speech or debating Buchanan's points, several students demanded that the campus police stop the event and declare it a "bias-related incident"—a punishable offense. The "Bias-Related Incidents Committee" ultimately declared the speech protected but then announced that it would explore developing policies that could prohibit similar future speeches. Outrageous though it seems, the students' reaction is understandable. Ithaca College teaches that it is okay to ban "biased" speech. The "Bias-Related Incidents Committee" shunned free speech as a sacred value and instead sought ways to punish disagreeable viewpoints in the future.

---

*Colleges must recognize that growth, progress, and innovation require the free and occasionally outrageous exchange of views.*

---

## Litigation Is Unnecessary to End Speech Codes

FIRE generally eschews litigation in favor of reasoning with campus administrators in detailed philosophical, academic, and moral arguments made in memorandums and letters. However, speech codes have proved remarkably impervious to reasoned arguments, for while FIRE often can snatch individual students from the jaws of speech prosecutions, administrators rarely abandon the codes themselves. (A happy exception was when in 1999 the Faculty Senate of the University of Wisconsin at Madison voted to repeal the longstanding code that restricted faculty speech.) FIRE thus initiated its litigation campaign.

Shippensburg is the beginning. In cooperation with FIRE's Legal Network, attorney Carol Sobel challenged a speech code at Citrus College, in California, where students were allocated three remote areas—less than 1 percent of the campus—for protest activities. Even if they were to protest within the ironically named "free speech area," students had to get permission in advance, alert campus security of the intended message, and provide any printed materials that they wished to distribute, in addition to a host of other restrictions. Further, this free-speech area was open only from "8 a.m. through 6 p.m, Monday through Friday." Citrus's student-conduct code banned "lewd, indecent, obscene or offensive conduct [and] expression," and included a number of other highly restrictive provisions. Just two weeks after the lawsuit was filed, the administration yielded and rescinded all of the provisions listed above. It is unfortunate that it took a lawsuit to demonstrate that restrictions on words have no place on the modern liberal-arts campus.

Colleges must recognize that growth, progress, and innovation require the free and occasionally outrageous exchange of views. Without speech codes, students are more likely to interact honestly. Having one's beliefs challenged is not a regrettable side effect of openness and intellectual diversity, but an essential part of the educational process. And, in fact, liberty is more than simply a prerequisite for progress; it is, at the deepest level, a fundamental and indispensable way of being human.

# The Use of American Indian Mascots and Team Names Should Not Be Banned

*Kenneth L. Woodward*

*Kenneth L. Woodward is a contributing editor at Newsweek magazine. Currently he is writing a history of American religion and culture since 1950.*

European intellectuals have long complained of excessive moralism in American foreign policy, politics and attitudes toward sex—the lingering effect, as they see it, of our Puritan heritage. But if they want to spot the real Puritans among us, they should read our sports pages.

[In August 2005], the National Collegiate Athletic Association [NCAA] announced that it would ban the use of Native American team names and mascots in all NCAA-sponsored postseason tournaments. If a team turns up wearing uniforms with words like "Indians," "Braves" or similar nicknames the association deems "hostile and abusive," that team will be shown the locker-room door. Surely I was not the only reader who noticed that this edict came out of the NCAA's headquarters in *Indianapolis, Indiana*.

Already, one university president, T.K. Weatherall of Florida State, one of 18 colleges and universities on the Association's blacklist, is threatening to take legal action—and I hope he does. Florida State's athletic teams are called the Seminoles, and the university says it has permission from that tribe in Florida to use that name. Not good enough, counters Charlotte Westerhaus, the NCAA's new vice president for "diversity and inclusion." "Other Seminole tribes," she claims, "are not supportive."

## The NCAA Is on a Moral Mission

One might suppose that any organization with an Office of Diversity and Inclusion would welcome mascots and team names reflecting the Native Americans among us. But no, the NCAA is on a moral mission—the less sensitive might call it a warpath—to pressure colleges and universities to adopt its standards for iconic correctness. Cheered on by moralizing sportswriters like George Vecsey of the *New York Times*, Jon Saraceno of *USA Today* and the entire sports department of the *Portland Oregonian*, which will not print "hostile" nicknames of teams (e.g., it calls the Washington Redskins "the football team from Washington"), several member schools have already caved in.

Stanford was the first major university to drop Indians as its athletic moniker; that was 30 years ago, when group identities and sensitivities were the most inflamed. Stanford's teams are now the Cardinals, presumably for the color of their jerseys. But who can tell?—it may have hidden ecclesiastical connotations. Marquette changed from Warriors to Golden Eagles, despite continuing complaints from alumni who find it as difficult as I do to imagine why the Warrior image would offend any Native American. After all, their forefathers weren't wimps.

Perhaps the most craven decision was that of St. John's University, which changed from the Red Men to the Red Storm. In both its former and current names, "Red" referred to the color of the St. John's uniforms—not to Native Americans, of which there are very few in Queens, N.Y. The change is reminiscent of a decision by Cincinnati's pro baseball team, which changed its name from Reds to Redlegs during the McCarthy hearings in the 1950s.

Interestingly, the NCAA has made an exception for the Braves of the University of North Carolina-Pembroke because the school has a tradition of enrolling Native American students. Maybe this will clear the way for Dartmouth's Big Green to restore its Indian mascot and team name, Indians, which

*Both the NCAA and professional sports leagues have adopted differing criteria for what teams can and should be named. This button protests the use of the Cleveland Indians mascot, Chief Wahoo.* Getty Images.

the school dropped in 1969. After all, Dartmouth was founded by Eleazar Wheelock, a Puritan minister, for the purpose of providing "Christianization, instruction and education" for "Youth of the Indian Tribes of this Land . . . and also of English Youth and any others." The college still offers a major in Native American Studies and since 1970 has graduated some 500 American Indians.

*Moralistic sportswriters need to distinguish between Native American activists and paternalistic surrogates.*

## The Moralizing of Sportswriters

The NCAA, thank God, has no control over pro sports teams and their chosen totems. But among sportswriters there are voices that echo the same faux moralizing by demanding name changes from the Atlanta Braves, Golden State Warriors, Kansas City Chiefs, Chicago Blackhawks and Cleveland Indians. In a typical column, Mr. Saraceno recently lamented the abject failure of "activists" to get Cleveland's baseball team to drop its logo, Chief Wahoo, which, he opined, "is probably the most outrageous, blatant symbol of racism in sports today."

I don't know where Mr. Saraceno was in the early '60s, when racism wore a human face. I was a civil-rights reporter in Nebraska then and remember visiting American Indian reservations where I saw kids wearing caps festooned with the Milwaukee Braves' logo and—yes—with Chief Wahoo. In 2002, *Sports Illustrated* published a survey of American Indians living on and off reservations. More than eight in 10 approved the use of Indian names and mascots for college and pro teams; a slight majority even approved of the clearly questionable "Redskins."

> If the NCAA and other latter-day Puritans are concerned about social prejudice, they ought to investigate Notre Dame.

Moralistic sportswriters need to distinguish between Native American activists and paternalistic surrogates. In Cleveland, for example Mr. Saraceno's unnamed activists are primarily officials of the United Church of Christ, an ultra-liberal Protestant denomination that moved its national headquarters there from New York in 1990 and immediately began a campaign against the Indians and Chief Wahoo. As it happens, the church is the denominational descendent of the old New England Puritans, now committed to diversity and inclusion. I was raised in Cleveland, and these interlopers don't seem to know or care that the baseball team took its current name in 1915 to honor popular outfielder Louis Sockalexis, a Penobscot Indian from Maine who batted .313 lifetime. His teammates called him "Chief."

# NCAA Mascot Policy Is Contradictory

As a matter of policy, the NCAA now encourages schools to imitate the University of Iowa, which won't allow its Hawkeyes to compete against nonconference schools that "use Native American nicknames, imagery or mascots," although "Iowa," itself, is a tribal name. Where does that leave the University of Illinois—a school in the same athletic conference, the Big 10—whose teams are called the Fighting Illini and whose gridiron mascot is Chief Illiniwek? Illiniwek—the word signifies "man"—was the name of an Indian confederation that the French called Illinois. If "the Fighting Illini" is "hostile and antagonistic" in the eyes of the NCAA, must the university, too, change its name? And the state as well? What about North and South Dakota? Or community colleges in Miami, Cheyenne, Pueblo and Peoria—Indian names all—not to mention a city named Sioux? Where do embedded history and folkloric iconography end and negative stereotyping begin?

Here's a suggestion: If the NCAA and other latter-day Puritans are concerned about social prejudice, they ought to investigate Notre Dame. Surely the name for its athletic teams, the Fighting Irish, is a slur on all Irish-Americans. The label derives from anti-Catholic nativists who reviled the poor and mostly uneducated Irish immigrants who came to these shores in the mid-19th century—a drunken, brawling breed, it was said, who espoused the wrong religion. When the fabled Four Horsemen played football for Notre Dame, the team was called the Ramblers. In 1927, the university officially adopted the Fighting Irish, thereby transforming a pejorative nickname into something to cheer about.

If there are Native Americans who feel that Indians or Warriors or Braves is somehow demeaning, they might reflect on the Notre Dame experience. And if the NCAA really cares about diversity and inclusion, it ought to establish an office of Indian Affairs to help Native American athletes with collegiate aspirations. Meanwhile, all paleface Puritan surrogates, beginning with the NCAA, should butt out.

# Restricting Internet Hate Speech Is Impossible

*Geoffrey Nunberg*

*Geoffrey Nunberg is an adjunct professor at the University of California–Berkeley School of Information Management and Systems. He is also a researcher at the Center for the Study of Language and Information at Stanford University.*

"What if the baseball could repair the window?" reads the headline of a recent ad for myCIO.com. The copy continues: "The Internet caused the problem. It's only fitting it should also provide the solution." As it happens, the advertiser is offering remote management of network security. But the slogan would serve just as well for dozens of other electronic products and services that promise to address the manifold anxieties that the Internet gives rise to—anxieties about hackers, threats to privacy, spam, rumors, commercialism, pornography, fraud, lost work time, or simply the difficulty of finding your way around cyberspace. For every article raising the alarm about one or another of these problems, there's a clutch of software engineers sitting in a loft somewhere trying to turn the concern into a market opportunity.

It's an understandable response, given the remarkable achievements of the technology and the hype that accompanies every new innovation. But it can also lead to misguided or even irresponsible decisions, as people naively trust the technology to right its own wrongs. It's one of the more dangerous guiding principles of the new economy: The remedy for the abuse of digital technology is more digital technology.

The problem is nowhere more evident than in the frenzy to equip homes, schools, libraries, and workplaces with blocking technology—the programs described as "content filtering software" by their makers and as "censorware" by their critics. They go by suggestive names like CYBERsitter, SafeClick, Cyber Patrol, NetNanny, SurfWatch, and I-Gear. It's a good business to be in right now. . . . Parents have been buying the software to protect their children, and search engines and Internet service providers (ISPs) have been offering blocking as a subscriber option. Corporations have been using the software to block employees' access to pornography (often citing the threat of sexual harassment charges) or, more generally, to restrict access to any non-work-related Web sites. Schools and libraries have been installing the software, sometimes reluctantly, in response to state and local laws that require its use, and federal legislation mandating filters is in the offing.

---

*The real scandal of the filtering controversy: The technology doesn't—and can't—work as promised.*

---

One reason for the enthusiasm about filters is that they can be seen as a benign alternative to legislative restrictions on speech or access. Such laws generally prove to be unconstitutional—like the Communications Decency Act, which was overturned in 1997. In fact, when the Third Circuit Court suspended enforcement of the 1998 Child Online Protection Act in February 1999, it cited filters as a less restrictive alternative. Advocates of filters argue that since the software is a commercial product that people adopt voluntarily, questions of censorship can't arise. As the director of one service provider that uses the software put it, "The First Amendment is not concerned with the capricious acts of individuals but rather with . . . the danger posed by the enormous power wielded by the federal government." . . .

## Blocking Software Cannot Work as Promised

Parental restrictions on children's access to information are clearly in a different category. As [former vice president] Al Gore frequently puts it, "Blocking your own child's access to offensive speech is not censorship—it's parenting." The problem is that parents who buy a commercial filtering program have no way of knowing exactly what speech it blocks, and the software companies are doing all they can to keep their customers in ignorance. The lists of sites blocked by most of the filters are kept encrypted, as are the keyword algorithms they use to block additional sites. And when free-speech advocates have hacked the filters and posted lists of the sites they block, the companies have gotten the courts to suppress the postings on the grounds that they violate provisions of the Digital Millennium Copyright Act. (Those provisions were relaxed [in] October [2000] to allow some circumvention of encryption mechanisms for purposes of finding out what sites filters are blocking.) All of this has put the censorware companies in a position that would delight any other business: Not only does government mandate the use of their products, it also enforces their right to conceal from the public what exactly those products do.

The software companies justify their secrecy by citing the need to protect their intellectual property and by arguing that publication of the lists of blocked sites would enable children to bypass the filters and access inappropriate materials. But neither argument is very plausible. Other companies manage to protect their rights to the databases they compile without keeping them secret, and it would be easy enough to make the lists publicly available without making them accessible to every schoolchild. The real danger for the software companies in making the lists public is that people would rapidly see just how inadequate their software is. That's the real scandal of the filtering controversy: The technology doesn't—and can't—work as promised.

Filters come in different forms. Some are implemented "upstream," at the level of proxy servers that control access for whole schools, libraries, or businesses; others are implemented "downstream" at individual workstations or PCs. But they all accomplish their filtering in pretty much the same way. The software companies start by compiling "control lists" of the addresses of unacceptable sites. Then, since these lists inevitably miss large numbers of offensive sites, they add automatic keyword filters to block additional sites that contain certain words and phrases. Most of them permit customers to specify the categories of sites they want to block—for example, "sex acts," "perversions," "hate speech," and "drug advocacy," not to mention additional categories like "job search," "games," and "dating," for the benefit of employers. (SmartFilter even adds a category of "worthless sites" that includes things like pages full of cat stories.) And most keep logs of use and make provision for automatic notification of parents or supervisors or system administrators when someone tries to access an excluded site.

---

*SurfWatch has blocked safe-sex information pages at Washington University, the University of Illinois Health Center, and the Allegheny University Hospitals.*

---

## Filters Block Too Much Information

The inadequacies of the systems are implicit in this basic architecture. In compiling their control lists, software makers have a natural interest in drawing the circle very broadly, so as to block sites that might be objectionable to one or another segment of their market, even if they wouldn't be considered pornographic or offensive by any reasonable standard. Take safe-sex information. SurfWatch has blocked safe-sex information pages at Washington University, the University of Illinois Health Center, and the Allegheny University Hospitals, and Cyber Patrol has blocked the HIV/AIDS information page of the *Journal of the American Medical Association* and the site of Planned Parenthood. SmartFilter blocks the safe-sex page of the Johns Hopkins Medical School research group on sexually transmitted diseases. The filters have also blocked numerous sites associated with feminism or gay and lesbian rights. Both I-Gear and CYBERsitter have blocked the site of the National Organization for Women (CYBERsitter cites the "lesbian bias" of the group). I-Gear has blocked the Harvard Gay and Lesbian Caucus, BESS has blocked the Gay and Lesbian Prisoner Project, and NetNanny has blocked Internet discussion groups on AIDS and feminism.

There's more: Many filters block Web privacy sites and sites that facilitate anonymous Web access. And filter makers routinely use their control lists to block sites critical of their products. SafeSurf has blocked the site of the Wisconsin chapter of the American Civil Liberties Union. I-Gear has blocked the site of the Electronic Privacy Information Center, and SafeClick has blocked some of the testimony at hearings on filters held by the congressionally appointed Commission on Online Child Protection. That must be the dream of every corporate publicist—to be able to prevent your customers from reading any negative comments about your products.

When we pass from control lists to keyword filters, we go from the outrageous to the ridiculous. Sites have been blocked simply because they contain the words *witch, pussycat,* or *button*. A government physics archive was blocked because its URL (uniform resource locator, or Web site address) began with the letters *XXX*. Keyword filters have blocked the sites of Congressman Dick Armey and Beaver College in Pennsylvania. What these anecdotes don't show, though, is just how extensive the overblocking of keywords is. The censorware companies like to claim that their accuracy is extremely high, citing library studies showing that inappropriate blocks constitute a tiny proportion of all Web accesses. For example, Secure Computing, the manufacturer of SmartFilter, claims that a Utah study showed that blocking of miscategorized pages by its program constituted only .0006 percent of all Web access attempts—a figure cited by Arizona Senator John McCain in support of a mandatory-filtering proposal he is sponsoring. But that's a highly misleading way of measuring overblocking: Even if a filter blocked every single site on the Web that mentioned safe sex or breast cancer, the total number of incorrectly blocked accesses would be tiny relative to the huge number of accesses to sites like Amazon.com and Yahoo! By analogy, imagine a police force that arrests every Arab American in town on an antiterrorism sweep, then claims that its false arrest rate is under 1 percent, since 99 percent of the total population was not detained.

## More Flaws in Filtering Systems

The only appropriate way to evaluate the filters is to ask what proportion of the sites they block as pornographic or offensive are in fact correctly categorized. And by this standard, the filters fare very poorly. In one recent study, 1,000 randomly chosen addresses in the dot-com domain were submitted to the SurfWatch filter. Of the sites it blocked as "sexually explicit," more than four out of five were misclassified—for example, the sites of an antiques dealer in Wales, a Maryland limo service, and a storage company in California. In another recent study, the free-speech advocate who runs *Peacefire.org* hacked the Symantec Corporation's I-Gear filter and published the list of the first 50 blocked URLs in the dot-edu domain. Fully 76 percent of these pages were errors or misclassifications, most of them completely devoid of sexual content of any kind. The program blocked a diagram of a milk pasteurization system with accompanying text entirely in Portuguese and two long sections of Edward Gibbon's *Decline and Fall of the Roman Empire.* It also blocked a tract by the seventeenth-century theologian John Owen entitled "Justification of Faith through the Righteousness of Christ" and a page that contained nothing but a passage in Latin from Saint Augustine's *Confessions.* (Intriguingly, it is a passage in which the bishop chastises himself for his impure thoughts—but the filter was doubtless triggered simply by the presence of the Latin preposition *cum.*)

This overblocking is an inevitable consequence of the keyword approach. The fact is, it's impossible to single out porn sites reliably simply by the words they use. Go to Disney's Go-.com, turn on the GoGuardian filter, and do a search on sex; you will get no hits at all. Then turn it off and discover what you were missing: not just porn pages, but the text of the *Scientific American* article "Bonobo Sex and Society," the pages on sex discrimination of the Australian Equal Opportunity Commission, and the Michigan Sex Offender Registry. It's true that filters can fare a bit better by looking for combinations of keywords and by doing some statistical analysis of content. But few of them appear to use sophisticated techniques, probably because any effort to reduce the number of false alarms will inevitably reduce the number of genuine porn or hate sites that they block as well.

Filtering advocates have argued that blocked Web pages on Saint Augustine or Gibbon are simply regrettable collateral casualties in the war against online porn and racism: Better, after all, to block some inoffensive sites than to allow some offensive ones to get through. As a field director of the profilter American Family Association puts it: "Filters are workable. We'd rather err on the side of caution instead of being too liberal." And there's no question that the software companies have deliberately kept their filters overly broad. It isn't just that they use overinclusive keywords like *sex* to screen out pages; they have also blocked whole servers or even whole ISPs when any one of their pages is flagged for objectionable content. Cyber Patrol blocked the entire Deja News (now Deja.com) site, which archives thousands of discussion groups on everything from commercial mortgages to archaeology, and all of the 1.4 million pages on the Web-hosting service Tripod.com. And a number of filters block pages containing banner ads that appear to contain links to inappropriate sites. The software makers reason, probably correctly, that their average customer is more likely to be concerned about porn sites that slip through the screen than about the blocking of useful sites—particularly since customers are usually ignorant about how frequently the latter occurs.

*A filtering company would require a full-time staff of more than 2,000 people just to check out the two million new pages that are added [to the Web] every day.*

## Programs Fail to Block Pornographic Sites

Yet even with the most overly restrictive filtering mechanisms, the programs don't do an adequate job of blocking porn and other offensive materials. You wouldn't know this from the claims of the software makers. CYBERsitter guarantees that its software blocks "more than 97 percent of all objectionable content" (though it doesn't define "unobjectionable"), and SurfWatch claims that it can "shield users from 90–95% of the explicit material on the 'net." But neither company says how it came up with these figures, and independent tests suggest that they are wildly exaggerated. A few years ago *Consumer Reports* tested the four most common filtering programs against a list of sites that its investigators judged clearly unsuitable for young children. SurfWatch blocked 82 percent of the sites, the highest score of the group, and CYBERsitter blocked only 63 percent (both programs performed much better than Net-Nanny, which blocked none at all). Another study showed that the filter BESS failed to screen out more than 275 of the sites identified as pornographic on Yahoo!—a singularly easy group to block, since they've already been located and labeled.

A study at the Annenberg School of Communications suggests that filters are even worse at identifying violent content than they are at catching pornography. That result is not surprising. Porn sites often give themselves away with genre-specific keywords like *XXX* or *cum*, and this makes for relatively efficient filtering. But the only way to block a large number of violent sites would be to use very general keywords that inevitably lead to the overblocking of thousands of useful or informative sites in the process. Do a Web search on "torture+domination," for example, and you will find a number of disturbingly lurid sites; but you will also find a report from the Canadian Centre for Victims of Torture, the summary of a human rights conference at the University of Chicago, and several pages documenting the horrors of the Holocaust.

What's more, these studies almost certainly underestimate just how leaky the filters are; and the proportion of offensive content that the filters miss will inevitably grow as the Web swells. For one thing, the filters simply can't keep up with the size of the Web and the vast amount of objectionable material it contains. In a 1999 article in *Nature*, Steve Lawrence and C. Lee Giles found that 1.5 percent of indexable Web servers contained pornographic material, a proportion that would translate to around 80,000 servers at the present size of the Web. Since a single server can host a number of sites, a highly conservative estimate would be 150,000 to 200,000 sites that contain pornographic material. These sites wink on and off and change addresses frequently: The archiving service Alexa-.com estimates that the average Web site has a life of 75 days. To locate and flag all this content, a filtering service would have to do periodic sweeps of the entire publicly accessible Web, which as of late 2000 contained in the neighborhood of 1.5 billion pages. That's more than anyone could possibly track: Even with the extensive resources that search engines like AltaVista and Inktomi have at their disposal, none of them indexes more than 15 percent of the total, and all of them taken together index less than half of it. And even if you could find all the Web pages, a filtering company would require a full-time staff of more than 2,000 people just to check out the two million new pages that are added every day.

# European Efforts to Restrict Hate Speech Are Totalitarian

*Sandy Starr*

*Sandy Starr is a public relations officer and writer for the British periodical* Spiked. *He also reviews books for the* Times Literary Supplement *(London), and reviews film and television for the British newspaper the* Sun.

The rush to find new legislation outlawing 'hate speech' on the internet has become a Europe-wide project. The 'Brussels Declaration' issued by the Organization for Security and Cooperation in Europe (OSCE)—which came out of the proceedings of its Conference on Tolerance and the Fight against Racism, Xenophobia and Discrimination, in which I participated in Brussels in September 2004—commits OSCE member states to 'combat hate crimes, which can be fuelled by racist, xenophobic and anti-Semitic propaganda in the media and on the internet.'

The chair of the European Network Against Racism, a prominent network of non-governmental organisations, argued at the same Brussels conference that 'any effective instrument to fight racism' in law should criminalise 'incitement to racial violence and hatred', 'public insults on the ground of race', 'the condoning of crimes of genocide, crimes against humanity and war crimes', 'the denial or trivialisation of the Holocaust', 'public dissemination of racist or xenophobic material', and 'directing, supporting or participating in the activities of a racist or xenophobic group'. Additionally, 'racist motivation in common crimes should be considered an aggravating circumstance'—as it already is in UK law.

Sandy Starr, "Why We Need Free Speech Online," *Spiked Essays*, May 26, 2005. Reproduced by permission.

As the idea that 'hate speech' is a growing problem in need of official regulation and censorship has reached prominence across Europe, it is not surprising that the internet has emerged as a particular focus for concern. . . .

---

*Initiatives to combat online hate speech threaten to neuter the internet's most progressive attribute—the fact that anyone, anywhere, who has a computer and a connection, can express themselves freely on it.*

---

## Regulating Internet Hate Speech Is Censorship

The internet continues to be perceived as a place of unregulated and unregulable anarchy. But this impression is becoming less and less accurate, as governments seek to monitor and rein in our online activities.

Initiatives to combat online hate speech threaten to neuter the internet's most progressive attribute—the fact that anyone, anywhere, who has a computer and a connection, can express themselves freely on it. In the UK, the regulator the Internet Watch Foundation (IWF) advises that if you 'see racist content on the internet', then 'the IWF and police will work in partnership with the hosting service provider to remove the content as soon as possible'.

The presumption here is clearly in favour of censorship—the IWF adds that 'if you are unsure as to whether the content is legal or not, be on the safe side and report it'. Not only are the authorities increasingly seeking out and censoring internet content that they disapprove of, but those sensitive souls who are most easily offended are being enlisted in this process, and given a veto over what the rest of us can peruse online.

## Regulation Proponents Are Disconcertingly Authoritarian

The Council of Europe's Additional Protocol to the Convention on Cybercrime, which seeks to prohibit 'racist and xenophobic material' on the internet, defines such material as 'any written material, any image or any other representation of ideas or theories, which advocates, promotes or incites hatred, discrimination or violence, against any individual or group of individuals, based on race, colour, descent or national or ethnic origin, as well as religion if used as a pretext for any of these factors'. Can we presume that online versions of the Bible and the Koran will be the first things to go, under this regime? Certainly, there are countless artistic and documentary works that could fall afoul of such all-encompassing regulation.

In accordance with the commonly stated aim of hate speech regulation, to avert the threat of fascism, the Additional Protocol also seeks to outlaw the 'denial, gross minimisation, approval or justification of genocide or crimes against humanity'. According to the Council of Europe, 'the drafters considered it necessary not to limit the scope of this provision only to the crimes committed by the Nazi regime during the Second World War and established as such by the Nuremberg Tribunal, but also to genocides and crimes against humanity established by other international courts set up since 1945 by relevant international legal instruments'.

This is an instance in which the proponents of hate speech regulation, while ostensibly guarding against the spectre of totalitarianism, are acting in a disconcertingly authoritarian manner themselves. Holocaust denial is one thing—debate over the scale and causes of later atrocities, such as those in the Sudan or the former Yugoslavia, and whether it is right to describe such conflicts in terms of genocide, is another, and there is an ongoing and legitimate debate about these issues. Yet the European authorities stand to gain new powers that will entitle them to impose upon us *their* definitive account of recent history, which we must accept as true on pain of prosecution. . . .

---

*Divvying up the principle of free speech in this way, so that especially abhorrent ideas are somehow disqualified from its protection, is a dubious exercise.*

---

## Limited Free Speech Is Not Free

Those who argue for the regulation of hate speech often claim that they support the principle of free speech, but that there is some kind of distinction between standing up for free speech as it has traditionally been understood, and allowing people to express hateful ideas. So when he proposed to introduce an offence of incitement to religious hatred into British law, former UK home secretary David Blunkett insisted that 'people's rights to debate matters of religion and proselytise would be protected, but we cannot allow people to use religious differences to create hate'.

Divvying up the principle of free speech in this way, so that especially abhorrent ideas are somehow disqualified from its protection, is a dubious exercise. After all, it's not as though free speech contains within it some sort of prescription as to what the content of that speech will consist of. Any such prescription would be contrary to the essential meaning of the word 'free'.

The Additional Protocol to the Convention on Cybercrime invokes 'the need to ensure a proper balance between freedom of expression and an effective fight against acts of a racist and xenophobic nature'. But this notion of 'balance' is questionable. Unless we're free to say what we believe, to experience and express whatever emotion we like (including hate), and to hate whomever we choose, then how can we be said to be free at all?. . .

## Distinguishing Speech and Action

The British academic David Miller, an advocate of hate crime legislation, complains that 'advocates of free speech tend to assume that speech can be clearly separated from action'. But outside of the obscurer reaches of academic postmodernism, one would be hard-pressed to dispute that there *is* a distinction between what people say and think on the one hand, and what they do on the other.

Certainly, it becomes difficult, in the absence of this basic distinction, to sustain an equitable system of law. If our actions are not distinct from our words and our thoughts, then there ceases to be a basis upon which we can be held responsible for those actions. Once speech and action are confused, then we can always pass the buck for our actions, no matter how grievous they are—an excuse commonly known as 'the Devil made me do it'.

It is not words in themselves that make things happen, but the estimation in which we hold those words. And if ideas that we disagree with are held in high estimation by others, then we're not going to remedy this situation by trying to prevent those ideas from being expressed. Rather, the only legitimate way we can tackle support for abhorrent ideas, is to seek to persuade the public of our own point of view, through political debate. When the authorities start resorting to hate speech regulation, in order to suppress ideas that they object to, this is an indication that the state of political debate is far from healthy.

> *The idea that we might regulate speech and prosecute crimes according to the emotions we ascribe to them, is one of the most totalitarian ideas imaginable.*

As well as distinguishing between speech and action, when assessing the validity of hate speech as a regulatory category, it is also useful to make a distinction between forms of prejudice such as racism, and generic emotions. Whereas racism is a prejudice that deserves to be contested, hatred is not objectionable in itself. Hatred is merely an emotion, and it can be an entirely legitimate and appropriate emotion at that.

When the Council of Europe sets out to counter 'hatred', with its Additional Protocol to the Convention on Cybercrime, it uses the word to mean 'intense dislike or enmity'. But are right-thinking people not entitled to feel 'intense dislike or enmity'? Hate is something that most of us experience at one time or another, and is as necessary and valid an emotion as love. Even David Blunkett, the principal architect of initiatives against hate speech and hate crimes in the UK, has admitted that when he heard that the notorious serial killer Harold Shipman had committed suicide in prison, his first reaction was: 'Is it too early to open a bottle?' Could he even say that, under a regime where hate speech was outlawed?

Hate speech regulation is often posited as a measure that will prevent society from succumbing to totalitarian ideologies, such as fascism. Ironically, however, the idea that we might regulate speech and prosecute crimes according to the emotions we ascribe to them, is one of the most totalitarian ideas imaginable. . . .

'Hate speech' is not a useful way of categorising ideas that we find objectionable. Just about the only thing that the category does usefully convey is the attitude of policymakers, regulators and campaigners towards people who use the internet. We are accorded the status of young children, uneducated, excitable and easily-led, who need a kind of parental control system on the internet to prevent us from accessing inappropriate content. The reaction to a few cranks posting their odious thoughts online is to limit all internet users' freedom about what they write and read. In seeking to restrict a communications medium in this way, it is the regulators who really hate speech.

# CHAPTER 4

# Current
## CONTROVERSIES

# How Can Hate Groups
# Be Stopped?

# Chapter Preface

Despite the efforts of federal, state, and local law enforcement agencies, nonprofit organizations such as the Anti-Defamation League and the Southern Poverty Law Center (SPLC), and community activist and school groups, the number of hate groups and Internet hate sites keeps growing. In 2005 the SPLC reported that the number of hate groups in the United States had reached an all-time high. From 2004 to 2005, the number of active hate groups rose by more than 5 percent—from 762 to 803 groups. This is more than a 30 percent increase since 2000, when the number of active hate groups was 602. Likewise, the number of hate Web sites has been growing. From 1998 to 2000, the number of these sites nearly doubled, jumping from 163 to 305. By 2004, the number had grown by over 50 percent to 468 hate sites. These sites play a significant role in the increase of hate groups because they act as veritable recruiting brochures for such groups.

Much of the increase in the number of hate groups comes from the white supremacist movement, particularly among its most violent strands—Racist Skinheads and Christian Identity. The former, who number forty-eight separate groups nationwide, are often referred to as the "shock troops" of their prophesied revolution. Christian Identity, whose member groups nationwide number twenty-eight, believe that whites, not Jews, are the true "chosen people" and that Jews are biologically descended from Satan. In 2005 the number of Ku Klux Klan groups increased by seventeen groups from the year before. The SPLC estimates that there are between fifty-five hundred to six thousand Klan members across the country. The increase in hate groups is also a reflection of the growth of antiwhite and anti-Semitic Black separatists. Currently, there are 108 such groups, whose numbers from 2003 to 2004 rose 66 percent, largely driven by the addition of more than thirty chapters of the New Black Panther Party. The authors in this chapter offer various ways to stop the growth of hate groups.

# Schools Can Prevent Hate Crimes

*Debra C. Cobia and Jamie S. Carney*

*Debra C. Cobia is a professor of psychology and Jamie S. Carney an associate professor of psychology at Auburn University in Alabama.*

Students are injured everyday in schools across the United States. Some of their injuries are physical, the result of serious violent crimes such as attacks with a weapon, sexual battery, rape, or robbery. For every 100,000 public school students in 1996–97, there were 26 attacks, 17 robberies, and 10 rapes reported in schools. Other less quantifiable injuries include the emotional distress and fear resulting from intimidation, harassment, racial/ethnic slurs and bigoted remarks, and threat of injury. Still others experience damage to their property through vandalism, theft, or graffiti. The "less violent" crimes reported in schools in 1996–97 totaled 952 per 100,000 students. Such incidents contribute to the creation of an atmosphere where some or many of the students feel threatened, unsafe, or unable to fully participate in the school environment.

## School Violence Is Motivated by Hate

As educators and others in society have struggled to understand and prevent school violence, a frightening common denominator has emerged. Many of these events are motivated by hate. The Anti-Defamation League defines a hate crime as one in which the victim is chosen based on his or her race, religion, sexual orientation, national origin, disability, gender or

Debra C. Cobia and Jamie S. Carney, "Creating a Culture of Tolerance in Schools: Everyday Actions to Prevent Hate-Motivated Violent Incidents," *Journal of School Violence*, vol. 1, no. 2, 2002. Copyright © 2002 by the Haworth Press, Inc.: Binghamton, NY. All rights reserved. Reproduced by permission.

ethnicity. Persons under 20 years old commit half of the hate crimes in the United States, and 10% of all such crimes are committed in schools and colleges. Unfortunately, some of the most injurious hate crime behaviors demonstrated by youth (e.g., the use of racial slurs) are not considered criminal acts. Nonetheless, name-calling, scapegoating, graffiti, harassment, and other forms of intimidation are clear examples of hate-motivated behaviors that are hurtful to the individuals and groups being victimized. Further, they are examples of incidents common to the school environment. . . .

## The Connection Between Intolerance and School Violence

Research indicates that many youth who are violent hold perceptions of others that are distorted by prejudicial attitudes and beliefs. [Researchers M.] Soriano, [F.] Soriano, and [E.] Jiminez have stated that "Racism, classism, sexism, and racial privilege" may all be linked to school violence. Bias-motivated behavior such as hate crimes are based on stereotyped, prejudicial, and intolerant views or attitudes about other cultural groups. In this context a culture includes the shared values, beliefs, forms of communication, norms, and attitudes of a group of people. The development of negative stereotyped attitudes or beliefs about persons from cultural groups other than one's own may begin early with preschool children already in the process of forming attitudes and beliefs about issues of race, ethnicity, and gender. Further, . . . students may establish their own peer cultures that are also defined by shared behaviors, values and attitudes. These peer cultures can influence attitudes and beliefs about other students and what are acceptable appearance, behavior, and interpersonal relationships. For many students their peer group culture may also influence attitudes and practices concerning violent behavior and tolerance.

# Columbine School Shootings

The risk of bias and prejudicial attitudes has been highlighted by [researchers K.] Dwyer et al., who identify biased attitudes and intolerance as one of the many early warning signs that a student may engage in school violence. These beliefs are often reflected in verbal or physical demonstrations of prejudice. For example, the perpetrators of the school shootings at Columbine High School in Colorado demonstrated biased beliefs and intolerance through class writings, videotapes, and on personal Web pages. Students who hold biased or prejudicial beliefs about other cultural or peer groups may seek out others with similar thoughts or even participate in organized groups that espouse these thoughts and beliefs. As well, some students who are the victims of bias-motivated violence may seek out opportunities to respond to their own abuse by harassing others or seeking violent means to protect themselves or strike back at injustices. For example, [Dylan] Harris and [Eric] Klebold, the Columbine shooters, talked of their resentment about being teased and bullied by their more popular classmates, particularly the athletes.

Without intervention, biased and prejudicial beliefs can negatively influence interpersonal relationships among youth, both within and outside of the school. Preliminary research indicates that these beliefs may play a significant role in the expression of verbal and physical aggression in the classroom. The results of a Harris Poll reported that nearly 75% of the students surveyed indicated that on a regular basis they had seen or heard about a racially motivated confrontation. In this same report one out of four of the students reported that they were the targets of these confrontations. Most startling was the finding that 47% of the students stated that they would participate in the confrontation, or at least condone it, because the victim "deserved" that attack. Another study reported that as many as 75% of the participating students had seen or heard a racially or religiously biased-motivated confrontation at school. The potential targets of hate-motivated violence in schools may be reflected in the results of the Met Life Teacher's Perceptions of Crime Survey; while the teachers in the sample indicated that they believed that schools were safe, they also identified the students they believed may be at increased risk for being victims of school violence. The students the teachers identified were students from lower socio-economic groups (22% of the teachers) and racial or ethnic minorities (15% of the teachers).

---

*In a recent study, 13% of students surveyed, ages 12 through 18, indicated that they had been targeted by hate language in schools.*

---

## Examples of Intolerance in Schools

The targets of hate-motivated behaviors reflect many of the groups that are targets of discrimination or victimization in our society, including gender, race, ethnicity, sexual orientation, socioeconomic status, and religion. As previously discussed, there are multiple ways that students may demonstrate their intolerance; one common method is through hate speech. In a recent study, 13% of students surveyed, ages 12 through 18, indicated that they had been targeted by hate language in school. In the same study 35% of the students reported seeing hate-related graffiti at school.

Within the school environment hate speech may take the form of name-calling, sexual taunts, racial slurs, or threatening statements. This type of verbal harassment is often the precursor to more physical forms of aggression, and sadly is all too easy for teachers and school administrators to overlook. In addition to words, hate speech may be represented by graffiti or in the images on students' t-shirts (e.g., Confederate flags, swastikas). Hate speech, such as that found in a symbol on a t-shirt, can create a hostile and threatening environment for specified groups of students even though there is no specific victim under attack. Although the First Amendment protects freedom of speech, hate speech of this nature is not protected and schools have a responsibility to protect students who are targets of this type of bias-motivated behavior.

## School Mascots Are Haters

One of the most graphic examples of hate speech is the continued use by some schools of mascots that reflect stereotyped depictions of non-majority groups such as Native Americans or symbols that are threatening to others (e.g., Confederate flags). These images and symbols are divisive and foster an environment that prohibits students from fully participating in the educational environment. While some have argued that these images reflect pride or honor, the use of stereotyped characterizations demonstrates a lack of knowledge of Native cultures and marginalizes those it seeks to "honor". In addition, these images may negatively affect the identity development of Native American children and adolescents within the school. The U.S. Commission on Civil Rights has called for an end to any use of Native American images and team names by all non-Native schools. To justify this decision the Commission stated that the use of such images in educational settings could potentially lead to the creation of a racially hostile school environment.

## Gays and Lesbians Targeted

Hate language is also a dominant feature of the harassment that students who are gay and lesbian face in schools. A recent survey found that 86% of students surveyed would be "very upset" if they were called gay or lesbian. This was the strongest response among males to the 14 different types of verbal harassment. This response in some part conveys attitudes students may hold towards gay, lesbian and bisexual peers. The negative feedback from other students about homosexuality and fear of physical assaults have led some gay students to make a decision not to disclose their sexual minority status at school. A significant number of gay and bisexual youth have experienced physical assaults at school, and many regularly receive verbal harassment. Others have experienced severe harassment, depression, anxiety and fear of attending school due to being harassed. Unfortunately, all too many gay and bisexual youth decide to run away, drop out of school or commit suicide to escape the harassment. Gays, lesbians, and bisexual youth are estimated to represent more than 30% of all adolescent suicides, and they have a significantly higher rate of suicide compared to other adolescents. A troubling aspect of this hate-motivated behavior is that in many instances schools overlook this form of harassment and are hesitant to develop programs which may address homophobic beliefs and practices. When schools choose not to respond to this type of school-based violence, one result may be the development of a hostile climate in which students are unlikely to seek assistance.

## Female Sexual Harassment

For many female students in our schools the experience of harassment is also all too real. [Researcher N.D.] Stein reports that this particular type of bias-motivated behavior is widespread throughout our elementary and secondary schools. Sexual harassment may involve sexual remarks and comments, sexual taunting, or physical groping, touching, or grabbing. There are estimates that as many as 80% of females have been sexually harassed at some time while in school, many prior to the third grade. In a study done by *Seventeen*, 89% of participants indicated that they had been sexually harassed; moreover, 39% stated that they were being harassed on a daily basis. The implications of this type of bias-motivated behavior can be pervasive and may only intensify the emotional and psychological issues females face in developing self-identity and self-worth. Furthermore, sexual harassment may negatively influence female students' academic and social development.

---

*Research indicates that teachers and other school personnel often do not respond to incidences of sexual harassment.*

---

## Schools Often Ignore Sexual Harassment

One of the most disturbing aspects of sexual harassment is that it often occurs in public situations in schools (e.g., classrooms, hallways) and in front of witnesses. In the *Seventeen* article, many study participants reported having been harassed in a classroom, and in one-third of those incidents a teacher witnessed the harassment. Research indicates that teachers and other school personnel often do not respond to incidences of sexual harassment. Stein reports that teachers may consider it part of males' normal development or "boys being boys," think that it is simply flirting or part of the interpersonal dynamics between male and female students, or convey that the female student in some way contributed to the behavior. When teachers and others in the school system ignore or minimize the significance of this form of harassment they are communicating acceptance, and creating an environment that is hostile to female students. In such an environment the academic, psychological, and emotional development of females is jeopardized. Finally, Stein cautions that by not responding, schools are helping to establish a pattern of violence in interpersonal relationships that may continue into adulthood.

## Intolerance of Racial Groups

Intolerance towards ethnic and racial groups appears to be a significant aspect of school violence. [Researcher D.] Harrington-Leuker suggests that while schools often deny that such tensions exist in their schools there are indications that racial and ethnic conflicts influence the school climate and the potential for school violence. Soriano, Soriano, and Jiminez cite the findings of a study among high school students in which 32% of the participants stated that a racially motivated incident had happened at their school. The numbers were higher for students at urban schools, 40% indicated that such an incident had occurred at their school, compared to 20% at rural schools.

## Muslim Victims of School Hate Crimes

Cultural and racial bias often reflects attitudes and ideologies in our society. Responses to the terrorist attacks on the World Trade Center in New York, New York, and the Pentagon in Washington, D.C., on September 11th, 2001, provide a context for understanding how significantly this relationship is influenced by societal factors and events. After the terrorist attack, many Muslim educators and Islamic schools were forced to deal with violence directed at individuals of Arab descent. This included harassing calls and the harassment of Muslim students. In schools across the United States students were harassed because of their real or presumed cultural heritage. In a California high school several students were named on a list that said the attacks on the World Trade Center would be avenged. The fear and anxiety this caused students and their families are common outcomes in bias-motivated hate crimes within schools.

Similar to other forms of hate-motivated incidences within the school, harassment towards ethnic and racial groups may include verbal harassment (e.g., slurs, jokes, graffiti) or physical assaults. The impact is significant and pervasive. In one court-reported case in which a ninth grade African American student was subjected to continued verbal harassment, the court stated that being verbally harassed and humiliated because of one's race, and having this harassment ignored by or rejected by her school, would undoubtedly negatively affect a child's ability to fully participate in or benefit from her academic experience. Others have also suggested that for many students existing in an environment that is hostile and marginalizes who they are can lead to academic failures, dropping out of school, and resentment, and may lead some to respond with violence. Furthermore, an environment that is hostile to diverse racial and ethnic groups is detrimental to the development of a healthy self and racial and cultural identity. The experiences of school violence victimization may be highest for African-American youths.

## Schools Often Unaware of How to Respond to Hate

Schools' responses to racially and culturally biased incidents have the potential to mediate the long-term implications of this type of school violence. However, there are indications that for some schools the response is one of denial or an unwillingness to respond. This may be based on a desire to distance themselves from the problem of school violence or a reflection of limited or no training on issues of cultural awareness and education. The impact of this lack of understanding about cultural differences may be best demonstrated by examining some of the strategies used to address school violence. For example, it has been suggested that zero tolerance programs that rely on the use of suspensions and expulsions may be over-identifying non-majority adolescents for this type of punishment. There is research, which indicates that African American students are only 17% of public school students but they make up over 32% of all suspensions. Others have also suggested that many of the methods used to prevent school violence are all too intrusive (e.g., searches) and all too often "disproportionately impact students of color".

Increasing diversity in schools may result in greater differences in the economic, interpersonal, family practices, and social aspects of students' lives. While cultural diversity cannot be considered the cause of bias-motivated aggression, as schools become more culturally and linguistically diverse, the potential for conflict rooted in bias and prejudice also increases. Understanding and responding to the needs of a culturally diverse student population, including the need to promote respect and understanding of individual and group differences, is essential if schools are to deal with the challenges associated with bias-motivated school violence.

## Comprehensive Approach to School Violence

There is broad consensus that effective school based prevention programs are comprehensive and include efforts aimed at prevention, intervention, and treatment. The suggestions we offer are aimed at both prevention and intervention and are proposed here as one component of a comprehensive violence prevention program that would also include school safety and crisis response initiatives. Although we are primarily concerned with those efforts that challenge prejudices and stereotypes which, if ignored, can lead to violent acts of hate, we recognize the need for and endorse a comprehensive approach to the problem of school violence.

---

*In order to fight bigotry, schools must convey the seriousness of their intention to stop any hate-motivated incident.*

---

## Most Schools Enforce Anti-bias Policies

School policies reflect the values of the school and serve as the foundation for a culture in which hate-motivated behaviors are either allowed to exist or are prohibited. In order to fight bigotry, schools must convey the seriousness of their intention to stop any hate-motivated incident. An examination of school policies with the goal of revising, rescinding, or replacing those that foster or maintain prejudices is an important first step. The publication, "Responding to Hate at School" published by the Southern Poverty Law Center (SPLC) offers concrete suggestions for developing anti-bias policies. Policies that promote tolerance, including the consequences for anti-bias acts, need to be discussed, posted on school web pages, displayed in hallways, and published in student handbooks to insure that all students and parents are aware of the policies and appreciate the value placed on them by the school.

Many schools already have in place anti-bias policies that forbid discrimination against or harassment of others, employees and students, on the basis of gender, race, ethnicity, age, religion, disability, marital status, and in some instances, sexual orientation. Such policies often include the specific types of discriminatory and harassing practices that will not be tolerated (e.g., comments that intentionally demean others). Additionally, the right to equal access to educational opportunities and to be treated with respect may be included. Such policies are typically congruent with the mission statement of the school system. To combat hate, broad policies to address hate crimes in the institution, a clear set of definitions related to hate symbols and language in the schools, programs to promote understanding and resolve conflicts, and training and orientation among employees and staff are suggested. . . . Standard policies found in violence prevention programs also include prohibitions against fighting and the precursors to fighting such as name calling; wearing gang colors and displaying gang symbols; clothing so oversized that weapons could be easily concealed; carrying weapons; and, graffiti and vandalism. Obviously, policies are driven in part by the needs and circumstances found in the community. There may be no need for statements about gang colors and symbols in communities where there are no gangs. . . .

The problem, . . . is not writing the necessary policies; the challenge for school systems is living them. Specifically, schools must have procedures in place for operationalizing policies related to tolerance or risk establishing or maintaining a climate where hate can take root and grow. Thus, it is important for all faculty and staff to model the values of tolerance for students. [Researcher J.] Drips states,

> Live the concepts stated for your school district. Do not let the concepts of acceptance, support, tolerance, and opportunity become hypocritical to any of your staff or students. State your beliefs over and over, as loud and as often as possible. Make them what you say they are—the cornerstone of policy and belief in your school system.

The beliefs must be reaffirmed each year as a new group of students, teachers, and staff arrive at the school.

## Sending a Message to Students

The way schools respond to bias-motivated incidents sends a message to all students about whether or not such behavior will be tolerated. Therefore, discipline policies to address hate-motivated incidents must be applied consistently and fairly. Seeking student input about possible consequences for bias-motivated behaviors that hurt others may serve the dual purposes of identifying consequences that may be incorporated into discipline policies and lead to group discussions that increase all students' awareness of subtle and overt forms of prejudice that are hurtful to others. The SPLC recommends involving the family of the offender(s) by inviting them to school and describing the offensive behavior and explaining why the behavior is unacceptable. A balanced approach to discipline involving the previously specified "punishment" coupled with a more affirmative measure such as a requirement for community service is also advocated.

Educators are challenged to respond to offenders such that the act(s) will not be repeated *and* offender's attitudes about the group targeted by the violence are changed. Some suggestions for doing so include involving a teacher or other adult whom the offender respects in the disciplinary conference. A well-known, respected adult may be able to influence the attitudes and behavior of the offender in ways that other staff cannot. Other strategies aimed at changing attitudes, such as learning about the group being maligned, may also be useful.

---

*When hateful acts occur in the school or community, schools are encouraged to act quickly to denounce the hateful act.*

---

## School Community Interventions

Creating a culture of tolerance may include, but is not synonymous with, multicultural education. Whereas a multicultural curriculum is designed to accurately portray the role in, and contributions to, society by all cultural groups represented, tolerance or anti-bias education is intended to reduce prejudice and discrimination toward these groups. The Anti-Defamation League identifies 101 strategies teachers and parents may use to combat prejudice. Some examples of those specific to schools include:

- Efforts to involve all members of the school community in developing policies and procedures that reflect a commitment to tolerance (e.g., form committees to develop rules of respect for school, including prohibition for hate speech and symbols and display them prominently in every classroom).

- Activities designed to increase awareness of the school's commitment to tolerance (e.g., create an anti-prejudice slogan for the school and feature it prominently [bumper stickers], write a school song about diversity, hold a poster contest, school plays and musical performances that are culturally diverse, post list of pioneers and leaders in each school subject with emphasis on diversity).

- Integrate diversity issues into school subjects on a daily basis (e.g., research peace negotiations around the world and stage a mock summit of world leaders, research civil unrest in the United States, hold a career fair with persons who can discuss diversity in their fields, invite college representatives to discuss diversity on campus, host a school exchange program to bring more diversity to each school).

- Bring focused attention to the negative outcomes of overt and covert expressions of prejudice (e.g., invite speakers on civil rights, organize essay contests around themes of experience with prejudice or fight against it, establish diversity clubs).

Other authors suggest interventions such as the integrated services models approach advocated in school reform movements of the 1990s that emphasize the cultural strengths of the family and professional and institutional collaboration; the creation of caring learning environments, sense of community, peer mediation programs, peer and cross-age tutoring programs, cooperative learning, and teacher advisor programs; and, the use of culturally sensitive behavior management strategies and promotion of involvement of culturally and linguistically different families.

Additionally, when hateful acts occur in the school or community, schools are encouraged to act quickly to denounce the hateful act. The SPLC recommends that schools issue a statement immediately to students and the media, denouncing the hateful act and reaffirming the school's position regarding respect and safety for all students. Additional statements are released as needed in order to inform students, parents, and faculty and staff of the progress of the investigation into the hate-motivated incident and to reassure everyone that appropriate measures to insure safety are being taken.

## In-School Interventions

[Researchers H.J.] Willert and [R.F.] Willert urge schools to use their greatest resource, teachers, to combat school violence by encouraging them to use collaborative learning and social skills training in the classroom. Both of these teaching strategies have the potential to create learning environments where students work together to solve problems. They listen to and learn from each other. Willert and Willert suggest that such strategies may humanize the relationships among students of diverse backgrounds and increase their willingness to accept differences, rather than devaluing each other. Additionally, all students need to learn to manage conflicts in a peaceful, nonviolent way. . . . [Other experts] advocate structuring academic controversies as one way to teach students to listen to, respect, and respond appropriately (nonviolently) to conflicts arising from different cultural perspectives.

Teachers are uniquely positioned in student's lives as they are among the few adults who may see a given student every day. Consequently, they are most likely to notice signs of student alienation and to witness hate-motivated behaviors that lead to isolation. Specifically, they may observe taunting and teasing, bullying, lack of involvement in social activities on the playground or in the cafeteria, lack of participation in extracurricular activities such as organized clubs, signs of prejudice or victimization expressed in written assignments, and absence of recognition for achievements of students from traditionally marginalized groups. The creation of a classroom environment where teasing, harassment, hate language and symbols, and bullying are not tolerated and where all students are encouraged to participate is the responsibility of individual teachers. Policies and procedures may provide guidance; however, the attitudes and behaviors modeled by individual teachers will have far more impact. Calling attention to and denouncing prejudicial behavior in all of the forms we have discussed leads to the development of a classroom environment where students feel safe, respected, and able to learn. In addition to stopping hateful expressions from students, educators are challenged to respond to bigotry from colleagues. According to the SPLC, teachers have ". . . a responsibility to intervene whenever the attitudes or actions of their colleagues jeopardize the welfare of any student. Teachers whose biases go unchallenged can easily apply or transmit these attitudes to students or be insensitive to expressions of bias in the classroom".

Teachers, particularly white teachers, are also challenged to examine their own assumptions about race and culture. [J.E.] King suggests that white teachers need to recognize and confront issues concerning their own biases and privilege. Additionally, all teachers need to learn about, and share with students, their cultural heritage. To serve more effectively as role models, teachers may stretch their own cultural comfort zone by expanding their current preferences for books, music, and art to include those representing the talents of many cultural groups. King also advocates that white teachers talk about issues of race and culture with students, nurture professional relationships and communicate with colleagues and students of color, and resist cynicism.

## Practicing Tolerance

The relationships between intolerance and hate-motivated violent incidents in school are becoming clearer. The most common forms of hate-motivated events, hate language, symbols, harassment, and other forms of racial and cultural discrimination are known to be precursors to the more physically injurious behaviors we typically identify as school violence. Unfortunately, these less violent precursors are frequently overlooked or ignored in schools even though many have policies expressly prohibiting them. In order to promote school cultures in which all students feel safe and free to participate fully in the educational enterprise, schools must fully operationalize their policies by providing clear and consistent guidelines for acceptable behavior and the consequences for violations.

School-wide practices that emphasize respect and safety, and individual responses promoting tolerance and denouncing prejudice by teachers and others in the school setting need to be demonstrated daily, not just during designated "diversity" weeks or months during the academic year. In order to practice and model tolerance, educators must examine their own attitudes and behaviors toward all groups of students to uncover any hidden biases that may prevent them from identifying and responding to gestures of hatred directed toward any of the groups we have discussed. Most importantly, educators must acknowledge that victims and perpetrators alike interpret silence in the face of expressions of prejudice as complicity.

# Communities Can Stop Hate Groups

*Southern Poverty Law Center*

*The Southern Poverty Law Center was founded in 1971 as a small civil rights law firm. Located in Montgomery, Alabama—the birthplace of the civil rights movement—the center is internationally known for its tolerance-education programs, its legal victories against white supremacists, and its tracking of hate groups.*

Hate in America is a dreadful, daily constant. The dragging death of a black man in Jasper, Texas; the crucifixion of a gay man in Laramie, Wyo.; and post-9/11 hate crimes against hundreds of Arab Americans, Muslim Americans and Sikhs are not "isolated incidents." They are eruptions of a nation's intolerance.

Bias is a human condition, and American history is rife with prejudice against groups and individuals because of their race, religion, disability, sexual orientation or other differences. The 20th century saw major progress in outlawing discrimination, and most Americans today support integrated schools and neighborhoods. But stereotypes and unequal treatment persist, an atmosphere often exploited by hate groups.

When bias motivates an unlawful act, it is considered a hate crime. Race and religion inspire most hate crimes, but hate today wears many faces. Bias incidents (eruptions of hate where no crime is committed) also tear communities apart—and threaten to escalate into actual crimes.

According to FBI statistics, the greatest growth in hate crimes in recent years is against Asian Americans and the gay and lesbian community. Once considered a Southern phenomenon, today most hate crimes are reported in the North and West.

And these numbers are just the tip of the iceberg. Law enforcement officials acknowledge that hate crimes—similar to rape and family violence crimes—go under-reported, with many victims reluctant to go to the police, and some police agencies not fully trained in recognizing or investigating hate crimes.

All over the country people are fighting hate, standing up to promote tolerance and inclusion. More often than not, when hate flares up, good people rise up against it—often in greater numbers and with stronger voices. . . .

Our experience shows that one person, acting from conscience and love, is able to neutralize bigotry. Imagine, then, what an entire community, working together, might do. . . .

## Do Something

"A hate group is coming to our town. What should we do?"

"I am very alarmed at hate crimes. . . . What can I, as one person, do to help?"

"I find myself wanting to act, to show support for the victims, to demonstrate my anger and sorrow. . . . But I don't know what to do or how to begin."

---

*Hate is an attack on a community's health.*

---

You probably want to "do something" about hate. You are not alone. Questions like these arrive daily at the Southern Poverty Law Center. When a hate crime occurs or a hate group rallies, good people often feel helpless. We encourage you to act, for the following reasons:

Hate is an open attack on tolerance and decency. It must be countered with acts of goodness. Sitting home with your virtue does no good. In the face of hate, silence is deadly. Apathy will be interpreted as acceptance—by the perpetrators, the public and, worse, the victims. If left unchallenged, hate persists and grows.

Hate is an attack on a community's health. Hate tears society along racial, ethnic, gender and religious lines. The U.S. Department of Justice warns that hate crimes, more than any other crime, can trigger larger community conflict, civil disturbances and even riots. For all their "patriotic" rhetoric, hate groups and their freelance imitators are really trying to divide us; their views are fundamentally anti-democratic. True patriots fight hate.

Hate escalates. Take seriously the smallest hint of hate—even what appears to be simple name-calling. The Department of Justice again has a warning: Slurs often escalate to harassment, harassment to threats and threats to physical violence. Don't wait to fight hate.

## Make a Call

When a cross was burned in the yard of a single mother of Portuguese descent in Rushville, Mo., one person's actions set in motion a community uprising against hatred.

"I have been asked many times since that night why I got involved," Christine Iverson said. "The answer is simple. I was so upset after reading the article that I had to do something. So I got up and made a phone call. Everything else came from that moment of decision."

Iverson, a disaster response expert and minister for Lutheran Social Services, called a friend involved in the church's anti-racism program. Then she called the victim. Then she called a ministerial alliance and asked to be put on the agenda. She went to the meeting with four proposals: a letter to the editor, a prayer meeting, flier distribution and a candlelight vigil. The alliance recommended all four, and Iverson was put in charge.

The result was a gathering of 300 people, a speech by the mayor, news accounts of the rally, and the formation of a unity committee within the church alliance. More than 150 people marched for the first time in a Martin Luther King Day parade, and an essay contest was created on the theme "We Have a Dream."

"There is still a lot of work to be done," Iverson said, "but we are beginning to do the work together." . . .

---

*A hate crime often creates an opportunity for a community's first dialogue on race, homophobia or prejudice.*

---

## Unite and Organize

Others share your instinct for tolerance. There is power in numbers in the fight against hate. Asking for help and organizing a group reduces personal fear and vulnerability, spreads the workload and increases creativity and impact. Coalitions for tolerance can stand up to—and isolate—organized hate groups. You and your allies can help educate others as you work to eradicate hate.

A hate crime often creates an opportunity for a community's first dialogue on race, homophobia or prejudice. It can help bridge the gap between neighborhoods and law enforcement. More people than we imagine want to do something; they just need a little push. As the creator of Project Lemonade [see below] found, "There are plenty of people of good conscience out there."

## Ideas to Start

Not sure where to start? Here are some ideas:

- Call the circle around you, including family, neighbors, co-workers, people in your church, synagogue or civic club. Meet informally at first.

- Call on groups that are likely to respond to a hate event, including faith alliances, labor unions, teachers, women's groups, university faculties, fair housing councils, the "Y" and youth groups. Make a special effort to involve businesses, schools, houses of worship, politicians, children and members of minority and targeted groups.

- Also call on local law enforcement officials. Work to create a healthy relationship with local police; working together, human rights groups and law enforcement officials can track early warning signs of hate brewing in a community, allowing for a rapid and unified response.

- Go door-to-door in the neighborhood targeted by a hate group, offering support and inviting participation in a rally, candlelight vigil or other public event. Put up ribbons or turn on porch lights as symbolic gestures. Declare a "Hate Free Zone" with a poster contest and a unity pledge. Set up a booth in a local mall to collect signatures on the pledge. Buy an ad to publicize the pledge and the contest winners.

- Fashion an appropriate, local response, but gather ideas from other towns that have faced hate events. . . .

## Project Lemonade

Bill and Lindy Seltzer, a Jewish couple in Springfield, Ill., were frustrated that the First Amendment gave neo-Nazis the right to march in public rallies. So they devised a way to turn hate's sourness into something sweet. Project Lemonade, now used in dozens of communities across the country, raises money for tolerance causes by collecting pledges for every minute of a hate-group event.

The Seltzers organized their first Project Lemonade during a 1994 Ku Klux Klan rally in Springfield. Using school equipment, they copied and mailed thousands of pledge fliers. Then they held a press conference to announce the unique event. They raised $10,000. When *People* magazine picked up the story, the idea spread nationwide.

The Seltzers created a kit for other communities that included practical advice: "Schedule an organizational meeting with community leaders, arrange for a local telephone number and answering machine, recruit volunteers, raise seed money, carry a supply of cover letters and pass them out. Involve the police. Invite the media. Schedule press conferences. Try to be interviewed for radio and TV talk shows. Keep Project Lemonade in the media as much as possible."

Lindy also warned would-be organizers to expect hate calls. "Ignore them. Stay positive and respectful. Encourage people to stay away from the Klan rally; they are looking for a fight. The Klan will leave, and the community will have the last say. It will be a positive one."

In Coeur d'Alene, Idaho, for example, the $28,000 raised during one white-supremacist rally supported human rights causes. In Boyertown, Pa., Project Lemonade so irritated the Klan that the hate group threatened to sue organizers for raising money "on our name." Money raised there went for library books on black history.

## Every Second Counts

Keith Orr, an activist in Ann Arbor, Mich., used the Project Lemonade model to create an "Every Second Counts" campaign in response to a 2001 rally by the viciously anti-gay Fred Phelps.

Orr knew a direct confrontation would actually add fuel to Phelps's fiery hate speech, so instead, he sought pledges to support a local gay-advocacy group. With pennies and dollars coming from as far away as California and New Hampshire, Orr raised nearly $7,500.

Orr then helped people in Madison, Wis., organize a similar response to Phelps, raising $6,000 more for the local Gay, Lesbian and Straight Education Network.

As Orr said later: "Fred Phelps himself may as well have written the check. It was his bigotry that pushed people to give." . . .

## Not in Our Town

Christmas was just around the corner in 1993 when Billings, Mont., entered a white-supremacist hell. Jewish graves were vandalized. Native American homes were sprayed with epithets like "Die Indian." Skinheads harassed a black church congregation. But these events received scant notice—until 5-year-old Isaac Schnitzer's holiday peace was shattered.

On Dec. 2, a chunk of cinder block broke his upstairs window. The window displayed a menorah, a row of candles lighted at Hanukkah. Responding police urged his mother, Tammie Schnitzer, to take down all their Jewish symbols. She refused and said so boldly in a news story.

As if suddenly aware of hate in its midst, Billings responded. Vigils were held. Petitions were signed. A painters' union led 100 people in repainting houses. Within days, the town erupted in menorahs—purchased at K-mart, photocopied in church offices and printed in the *Billings Gazette* —displayed in thousands of windows.

Mrs. Schnitzer took her son for a ride through town to look at all the menorahs.

"Are they Jewish, too?" a wide-eyed Isaac asked.

"No," she said, "they're friends."

Rick Smith, the manager of a local sporting goods store, was so moved by events that he changed the sales pitch on his street marquee. Instead of an ad for school letter jackets, he mounted, in foot-high letters: "Not in Our Town. No Hate. No Violence. Peace on Earth."

The marquee got national exposure, and "Not in Our Town" became a famous slogan. It went on to title a Hollywood movie, a PBS [Public Broadcasting Service] special, a school musical and a tolerance movement in more than 30 states.

## The Ripple Effect

Not in Our Town, with its forceful message to hate groups, is now spread by The Working Group, a nonprofit production company that produced the video, "Not In Our Town." Subsequent videos show what communities around the country have done to fight hate.

Margaret MacDonald was among those who ignited the anti-hate movement in Billings. A decade after the events, she still is moved.

"The story of Billings embodies how people believe the world ought to be," she said. "It touches on First Amendment responsibilities (and) civic responsibility; it's about multiple faiths finding ways to validate each others' liberties and freedoms. It's a transformation of violence and hate into peacemaking." . . .

## An Alternative to Hate in Maine

On Oct. 1, 2002, the mayor of Lewiston, Maine, sent an open letter to the town's growing Somali community. He told them the town was "maxed-out, physically and emotionally" from what the press began to call a Somali "invasion."

By that point, about 1,100 Somali immigrants lived in Lewiston, a city of about 36,000 residents.

One Somali resident told a local newspaper he was shocked by the sentiment in the mayor's letter. "He thinks he's mayor for only white residents," Mohamed Driye said. "He's not only their mayor. He's our mayor, too." Others, in a letter, described the mayor as "an ill-informed leader . . . bent toward bigotry."

Two hate groups—the National Alliance and what was then known as the World Church of the Creator—saw an opportunity for "outreach." They planned a January 2003 rally in Lewiston, hoping to attract disgruntled, anti-immigrant residents. Their own "open" letter to the town began with this greeting: "Dear fellow white people."

Somalis and their many supporters in Lewiston planned an alternative event. Local churches, students and dozens of concerned residents joined the effort.

Working with hate-group experts, including the Southern Poverty Law Center, the group chose not to engage the hate groups directly, but rather to send a separate, stronger message against hate.

"We invited everyone together . . . and brought everyone under one umbrella," the Rev. Mark Schlotterbeck said.

Added James Carignan, a professor and dean at Bates College, referring to the planned hate rally: "This is not who we are, and we have to make sure people know that."

The umbrella group, calling itself the Many and One Coalition, planned teach-ins and a diversity rally for the same day, in a different location.

The result? More than 4,000 attended the Many and One event, while fewer than 100 showed up at the hate rally.

Ziad Hamzeh later made a film about Lewiston; "The Letter" has played at film festivals across the country, drawing praise and garnering awards.

---

*Hate usually doesn't strike communities from some distant place. It often begins at home.*

---

"I went to Lewiston thinking, 'What do these people have to teach me?' And they taught me a lot," Hamzeh said. "They taught me to be a better American, a better human being. I was able to relearn and re-experience again what America is."

## Hate Begins at Home

Hate usually doesn't strike communities from some distant place. It often begins at home, brewing silently under the surface. Hate can grow out of divided communities, communities in which residents feel powerless or voiceless, communities in which differences are the cause of fear instead of celebration.

The best cure for hate is a tolerant, united community. As Chris Boucher of Yukon, Penn., put it after residents there opposed a local meeting of the Ku Klux Klan, "A united coalition is like Teflon. Hate can't stick there."

Hate exists "because the ground in the area is receptive for it," says Steven Johns Boehme, leader of the Michigan Ecumenical Forum. "If you drop the seeds of prejudice in soil that is not receptive, they won't take root."

Experts say the first step in changing hearts is to change behavior. Personal changes are important—the positive statements you make about others, unlearning assumptions about people who are different—but community-wide changes are instrumental, too.

# Understanding the Psychology of Hate Groups Can Help Society Stop Their Growth

*Linda M. Woolf and Michael R. Hulsizer*

*Linda M. Woolf is a professor of psychology at Webster University in St. Louis, Missouri. Her research interests include hate groups, terrorism, and peace psychology. Michael R. Hulsizer is an associate professor of psychology at Webster University. His research interests include hate groups, mass violence, and international human rights.*

Hate does not exist in a vacuum. Rather, hate is learned, often from one's family, but also through the groups that one joins. Throughout the history of the United States the public has primarily associated hate groups with acts of hate and violence against individuals such as Matthew Shepard [a gay man murdered in Wyoming in 1998], and James Byrd [a black man killed in Texas in 1999]. However, hate groups have also been increasingly associated with a large number of domestic terrorist attacks ranging from church burnings to the bombing of the Federal Building in Oklahoma. Consequently, given the persistence of hate-related crime, violence, as well as terrorism, an exploration of the psychosocial functioning of hate groups is imperative.

There are several key aspects necessary for the successful creation of a hate group. It is important to recognize that hate itself is often more of a "means" than an "end" for these organizations and particularly their leaders. In other words, while hate may be the glue that binds and subsequently drives the organization, the motivations behind individual membership are typically grounded in psychological needs such as belong-

Linda M. Woolf and Michael R. Hulsizer, "Hate Groups for Dummies: How to Build a Successful Hate Group," *Humanity and Society*, vol. 28, no. 1, February 2004, pp. 41–62. Reproduced by permission.

ingness, status, recognition, and power. As such, it is possible to create enmity where none previously existed simply by utilizing a variety of psychosocial mechanisms and pairing these with historically inaccurate perspectives of specific minority groups. Therefore, we must understand the variables that allow for the creation of a hate group before devising strategies to reduce the effectiveness of such organizations. . . .

## How to Create a Hate Group

If we want to combat hate, it is imperative that we examine the psychological reasons that bring individuals to a hate group's doorstep, the mechanisms involved in getting them through the door, and the processes involved in organizing these individuals into a group committed to enmity. It is important to note that this discussion is not designed to be a "how to" book for the creation of a hate group. Rather, through an identification of the various factors designed to promote hate, we can work to counter such hate and endeavor to build communities that value diversity and the promotion of peaceful coexistence.

---

*In a sense, the hate group leader becomes a coach making members feel needed, valued, and efficacious as well as building a high level of loyalty to both the leader and the group.*

---

## Leadership Dynamics

At the core of any hate group exists a leader or leadership group. Without such leaders, it might be argued that a hate group would cease to exist. In other words, if one removes the head of the snake, the body will naturally die. Unfortunately, while leaders are necessary for the coordinated expression of hate, the survival of a hate group may depend less on the specific, idiosyncratic leader than on the presence of simply someone in a leadership position who has learned basic group dynamics. . . .

The most effective hate group leaders will engage in the following behaviors. First, any leader of a hate group must work to build their credibility within the group and reinforce the confidence of their followers regarding their leadership abilities. Effective image management will increase the ability of the leader to influence group member's behaviors as their followers will view the leader as trustworthy and competent. Second, hate group leaders need to understand the needs and abilities of their group. With this knowledge, they can most effectively manipulate the needs and wants of the group as well as best utilize the abilities of the group. In a sense, the hate group leader becomes a coach making members feel needed, valued, and efficacious as well as building a high level of loyalty to both the leader and the group. Finally, a hate group leader should be adaptive. As situations and contexts change, the most effective leaders can shift gears to get the maximum effort towards organizational success out of individuals and members of the group. Each of these characteristics can be applied to White Aryan Resistance (WAR) leader Tom Metzger. Metzger's leadership has taken him from California's Grand Dragon of the Knights of the Ku Klux Klan to a House of Representatives' Democratic nomination and finally as the leader of WAR. Through WAR he hosts a cable TV show, publishes a newsletter, and maintains an Internet web site. His leadership efforts have resulted in such influence and loyalty that skinhead followers have killed minority group members based allegedly on his coaching. . . .

## Exceptional Recruits

Hate groups not only need leaders but they need recruits. . . .

Methods of recruitment are often aimed at psychological needs. Thus, a lonely individual may be invited simply to a picnic drawing on their need for affiliation or a teen may be introduced to racist music or video games drawing on typical adolescent needs for entertainment and excitement. According to [researcher K.M.] Blee, most of the women in her research began to identify with a racist agenda only upon developing a social connection to members of the group. Thus, the development of a racist ideology was a consequence and not a cause of membership in a hate group. [Researchers Jack] Levin and [Jack] McDevitt discuss the "power of a tune to persuade" as well as the excitatory lure of the hate group for adolescents. Resistance Records offers a variety of racist rock music compact disks as well the video game, "Ethnic Cleansing: The Game". The description for the video available on the web site states that: "The Race War has begun. . . Not one of their numbers shall be spared." The goal of the game is to kill as many "subhumans" as possible, including Jews, Latinos, and Blacks.

## Us and Them

While personality factors may play a role in prejudice and more importantly provide reasons for joining a hate group, it is important to remember that other psychological factors play a major contributory role in the success of a hate group. In other words, while an individual may be predisposed to the draw of extreme prejudice due to personality or individual vulnerability, it is other social psychological mechanisms that lead an individual to not only join but also become a contributing member of a hate group. . . .

Researchers have also found that we tend to divide the world into us and them—ingroups and outgroups. However, this distinction between us and them is far from trivial. . . . It is advantageous for us to belong to groups that are held in high esteem so that we are seen in a positive light. Consequently, people try to sustain their positive social identity by assuring themselves that their ingroup is highly valued and distinct from other groups—a phenomenon referred to as the ingroup bias. For example, mythologies created by white supremacist organizations such as Aryan Identity or Christian

Patriots are designed to glorify those "chosen" as distinct from the "other" parasitic and degenerate "races". The ingroup bias, coupled with the outgroup homogeneity effect, the tendency to view outgroup members as similar and one's ingroup as diverse, add to the chasm that separates us and them. . . .

Individuals and/or groups may also go so far as to seek out information that confirms the superiority of their group over a specific outgroup—a phenomenon referred to as the confirmation bias. Blee discusses at length the ability of organized hate groups to teach individuals to filter their life experiences through the lens of racist principles. . . . Once these beliefs are formed, group members are extremely reluctant to modify them. This phenomenon, referred to as belief perseverance, can account for the tenacity with which hate groups hold on to their beliefs—regardless how illogical their beliefs. *The Protocols of the Elders of Zion*, a forged anti-Semitic document, continues to resurface and be used as evidence of a Jewish world dominance conspiracy thus "confirming" some of the base tenets of anti-Semitism.

## Internal Causes of Hate

Another bias that we use when processing information is the fundamental attribution error—the tendency for individuals to attribute behavior to internal, dispositional causes, ignoring situational explanations. Thus, individuals are more likely to believe that African-Americans make up a disproportionate number of individuals in prison because they are inherently "bad", "inferior", or "evil" as opposed to examining situational causes such as poverty, institutionalized racism, etc. The tendency for individuals to make the fundamental attribution error, coupled with their desire to believe in a just world, leads people to blame the victim for whatever unfortunate event has befallen them. For example, there are those that argue that the Jews brought the Holocaust upon themselves and others who attribute the 9/11 tragedy and the explosion of the space shuttle Columbia to God's anger at the state of America for its tolerance of homosexuality. . . .

## Pressure to Conform in Hate Groups

The nature of group dynamics within a hate group can further entrench individual hatred and greatly increase the likelihood of violence. For example, the organizational structure of a hate group, which can often be quasi-military, necessitates conformity to the group ideal. In addition, there are often very severe penalties for not conforming, ranging from ostracism and verbal aggression to physical violence. Thus, group members may initially feel pressure to engage in hatred and violence, knowing only too well the ramifications of not conforming. Later, after engaging in such acts, cognitive dissonance—the internal pressure to achieve consistency between our thoughts and actions—necessitates that members either internalize a rationale for their hatred of the outgroup or leave the hate group. The former option is much easier and thus much more likely to occur. . . .

Hate groups will often have new members engage in relatively innocuous activities such as simply setting up a literature table at a group event before moving on to greater levels of commitment. Such activities are met with acceptance, approval, and reward. Eventually, the adage of "in for a penny, in for a pound" applies as recruits are subjected to increasing levels of commitment, a push for conformity, and are driven to obey the leaders. In an attempt to avoid cognitive dissonance, recruits become increasingly committed to the hate group's ideology and activities, increasingly identified solely as a group member, and increasingly loyal to those in positions of authority. Blee identifies three levels of commitment that develop over time to racist groups: contact with the group, identification as a racist, and finally commitment to a racist activism.

## Hate Groups Strip People of Their Identities

Hate groups, not unlike other groups, tend to foster a sense of anonymity or deindividuation among members. Unfortunately, by stripping individuals of their identities through increased anonymity, deindividuation causes people to become less self-aware, feel less responsible for their actions, and be more likely to engage in violence if placed in a provocative situation. Consequently, tendencies towards hatred and violence are enhanced within hate groups that foster a sense of deindividuation.

As previously mentioned, hate groups often adopt a quasi-military structure that not only fosters deindividuation, but also compartmentalization of function and diffusion of responsibility among its members. Uniforms and clearly identifiable proscribed rules for behavior facilitate the processes of deindividuation, conformity, diffusion of responsibility, and ultimately violence if such behavior was dictated by those in positions of power. Whereas a local businessperson might never dream of killing someone as part of their daily life, they might easily engage in a lynching while wearing a robe and participating as a member of the group.

---

*The majority of hate crimes are committed by pairs or groups as opposed to lone attackers due to the increased anonymity, groupthink, diffusion of responsibility, and group justification.*

---

## Groupthink Fosters Group Harmony

Another factor that can increase the degree of enmity among hate group members is group polarization. Research has demonstrated that group discussion tends to enhance the initial leanings of groups that are composed of like-minded individuals. The same can be said of prejudiced individuals, who adopt much more negative views regarding outgroup members following group discussions. In addition, very cohesive groups tend to suppress realistic appraisals of the situation in order to maintain group harmony. The result is groupthink in which groups tend to agree with the leader and ignore possible alternative viewpoints. Thus, the potential exists within a very cohesive group for a leader to advocate a policy of extreme hate and even violence without being met by significant resistance from group members. In fact, group polarization may occur, resulting in even increasingly extreme viewpoints. . . .

The majority of hate crimes are committed by pairs or groups as opposed to lone attackers due to the increased anonymity, groupthink, diffusion of responsibility, and group justification. . . . These attacks are often more "thrill" motivated than grounded in well entrenched antipathy and if perpetrators are caught early they may be deterred from further destructiveness. Such a distinction highlights the impact of social psychological influences on hate-directed behavior. Unfortunately, individuals enmeshed within a hate group are unlikely to be discouraged from further violent actions against target groups and are in fact likely to be rewarded for such efforts. . . .

## Hate Groups Scapegoat Enemies

One of the means by which we assess our status in society is comparing ourselves to others. However, in comparing ourselves to those around us we may find that we are not achieving the same degree of success as our chosen comparison group. Consequently we may experience relative deprivation. Given that relative deprivation tends to lead to frustration, hate group members may elect to vent this frustration via displaced aggression or scapegoating. For example, the number of southern African-Americans lynched in the late 19th and early 20th centuries varied as a function of the price of cotton. When cotton prices were good, lynchings were down, whereas the opposite pattern held true when cotton prices were low. The researchers cited displaced aggression as the main culprit in this analysis. Groups that have a limited ability to defend themselves, such as women, children, and ethnic and religious minorities are often attractive targets. According to [researcher A.L.] Ferber, young white males are likely to join white supremacist groups because of the perceived futility of the American Dream. For example, Benjamin Smith, Matthew Williams, and James Tyler Williams all had ties to the white supremacist group, the World Church of the Creator. Smith went on a three-day shooting spree aimed at Blacks, Jews, and Asians and killing two, and the Williams brothers killed a gay couple and fire-bombed three synagogues in California. . . .

## Hate Groups Dehumanize Victims

To facilitate movement along a path of escalating enmity and potential violence, hate group leaders promote increasing levels of dehumanization. The process of dehumanization begins with increased promotion of stereotypes and negative images of the outgroup. This is often a necessary tool to reduce the cognitive dissonance that may occur when individuals behave negatively toward other human beings. Propaganda is a vital tool used by the ingroup elite to stigmatize and dehumanize the outgroup, as well as to present the outgroup as an imminent threat to the well-being or existence of the ingroup. The outgroup may be presented as being in partnership with the devil, as a seductive evil seeking to steal one's children, or as insects. For example, white supremacist web sites often contain images of Blacks, Jews, Hispanics, and others portrayed as demons, predatory animals, and vermin. These messages lead members down a path towards violence that includes increasing levels of devaluation and dehumanization of the "other." According to Blee such a culture of violence is normative for organized hate groups. Even the children in these groups are engulfed in a culture of hate propaganda ranging from refrigerator-posted pictures of lynchings and comic book depictions of Jews and Blacks as vermin to evenings of fun topped off by cross burnings.

The process of dehumanization and the path of violence could not be taken without the underlying processes of moral disengagement and moral exclusion. Over time, ingroups begin to view the outgroup as excluded from the ingroup's normal moral boundaries and disengage morally. In other words, certain moral principles that may be applied to one's own group do not pertain to those outside of the group. For example, it is unfortunate but acceptable to kill an enemy during war when the soldier is identified as a member of the threatening outgroup. Historically in relation to hate, this has been carried to the extreme with genocide. For example, during the Holocaust, as Jews were forced into ghettos and sent to concentration and death camps in unknown locations, many non-Jews began to disengage morally from Jews. Jews began to be perceived as not only "other" but excluded from the normal moral realm. In fact, Nazi propaganda argued for such disengagement and exclusion on the grounds that Jewish blood represented a threat to the body and survival of Germany....

## Communities Can Combat Hate Groups

Hate groups are unlikely to disappear from the landscape either in the United States or abroad in the near future. This does not mean, however, that individuals should simply ignore hate groups and hope that they go away. Historically, turning away from the face of hate has served as tacit approval for the existence of hate. Thus, it is imperative that intervention and prevention be discussed....

There are several steps that communities can take to combat enmity in the form of hate groups. First, as discussed previously, groups can be focused around either destructive or constructive agendas. Thus, groups aimed at the development of positive values and goals can be designed to meet some of the same psychological needs for belonging, value, status, etc. as hate groups. Often such options are not available or are not promoted in a way that makes these groups attractive to those who otherwise may feel disenfranchised. These groups and efforts are particularly important for youth, young adults, and during times of social, political, or economic crisis.

## Political Lobbying

Political lobbying in relation to hate groups also needs to be organized. This is imperative for three primary reasons. First, for the programs and community activities discussed above to happen, resources need to be committed for funding and staffing. Monies need to be especially allocated towards program recruitment. Unless individuals make it through the front door, they are unlikely to develop long-term associations and involvement with organizations designed with productive agendas. In other words, one needs to get that "foot in the door" with initial new members. Just as individuals can begin and move down a path of hate, violence, and destruction, research has demonstrated that individuals can just as easily move down a path of benevolence. Special effort needs to be directed towards connecting these organizations to and through the Internet. As noted previously, hate groups recruit on high school and university campuses as well as through the Internet, and thus, so should organizations designed towards more constructive values including those emphasizing diversity.

## Greater Focus on Education

Greater focus on education is also imperative both in our schools and our communities. Ten percent of all hate crimes in the United States occur in schools and universities. Additionally, as noted previously, children who develop prejudicial attitudes and biases are more likely to become adults with these same belief systems. Thus, schools and universities are natural environments for education about hate, tolerance, and diversity. Programs such as "A World of Difference" are a good place to begin for schools unfamiliar with diversity education. Additionally, as part of education, our youth need to be "inoculated" against potential recruitment. For example, researchers have successfully inoculated children against peer pressure to smoke and engage in drug use. Finally, it is important that not just positive self-esteem be developed in children and youth but self-esteem grounded in actual accomplishments and demonstrated abilities. . . . When threatened, false self-esteem is a source of potential violence as often evidenced in gangs and other destructive groups.

---

*Individuals who feel they have [been] left behind in the pursuit of the American Dream or feel otherwise disenfranchised are ripe recruits for hate-based organizations.*

---

## Pressure Government Officials

Furthermore, hate groups have operated in many areas around the United States with relative impunity as some governmental officials have turned a blind eye to hate group activities. Local elected officials and law enforcement officials are not exempt from holding belief systems grounded in hate. However, communities can put political pressure on these individuals to hold them to broader community values of tolerance and acceptance of diversity. As hate groups become identified as a source of shame as opposed to power and prestige, they fade from the community landscape. Finally, concern for hate group activity is often diminished as officials are unaware of the interrelationships between hate group organizations and their leaders. Unfortunately, this lack of awareness has led to instances in which law enforcement officials were caught unprepared for the risk and reality of violence. Thus, local and national need to be lobbied for increased tracking of hate group activity to assess risk for violence.

Additionally, we must address some of the underlying problems in society that lead many individuals to groups grounded in enmity. Issues such as poverty, unemployment, illiteracy, housing, etc. may all seem tangential to the issue of hate. However, individuals who feel they have [been] left behind in the pursuit of the American Dream or feel otherwise disenfranchised are ripe recruits for hate-based organizations. During the farm crisis of the late 1970s, many farmers and others in farm regions of the United States joined the Posse Comitatus and other hate groups as they felt no others were concerned or provided solutions to their life difficulties.

Finally, it is important to bear in mind that modern prejudice and racism is prevalent in everyday society and does not simply exist within the hate group. The cabbie that refuses to stop to pick up a young Latino, the police officer who polls over a vehicle simply because the occupants are Black, or the employer who promotes the male applicant over the more qualified female applicant are all examples of the effects of modern day prejudice and discrimination in everyday life. If hate is to be truly tackled in the United States as well as around the globe, the issue of everyday prejudice and hate as well as organized enmity must be addressed.

# The United States Should Support Great Britain's Crackdown on Hate Groups

*Nile Gardiner*

*Nile Gardiner is a fellow at the Margaret Thatcher Center for Freedom and a fellow in Anglo-American Security Policy at the Heritage Foundation, a nonprofit research institute in Washington, D.C.*

British Home Secretary Charles Clarke [in August 2005] declared his government's intention to deport or exclude individuals who advocate or support the use of terrorism. Clarke outlined a list of "unacceptable behaviors" for foreign nationals. It includes the expression of views that "foment, justify or glorify terrorist violence in furtherance of political beliefs" or "seek to provoke others to terrorist acts." This covers "any means or medium," including publications, public speaking, preaching, websites, and positions of responsibility such as teaching or community leadership.

Publication of the list has sent a clear warning to advocates of terror, especially radical Islamic clerics, that they will no longer be tolerated on British soil and that they will face the full force of British law. The British government recently detained ten foreign nationals on national security grounds and is likely to begin deportations in the next few days. It is in the process of negotiating a series of agreements with North African and Middle Eastern governments on the deportation of terror suspects and has sought guarantees that deported individuals will not be subjected to torture or inhumane treatment.

Nile Gardiner, "The U.S. Should Strongly Support Britain's Anti-Terrorist Measures," Heritage Foundation, August 26, 2005. Reproduced by permission.

## London Bombings

The new deportation rules, which have the support of the opposition Conservative Party, are part of a powerful array of anti-terror measures to be formally introduced in coming weeks. Formulated in response to the July 7 [2005] London bombings that killed 52 people and injured hundreds, they will be a vitally important asset in Britain's war against Islamic terrorism.

They include the banning of [hate] groups such as Hizb ut Tahrir and its successor Al-Muhajiroun, a tightening of both asylum and citizenship laws, the possible closing of mosques found to be harboring extremists, an increase in the number of special judges dealing with terror cases, the introduction of biometric visas, and the creation of a database of foreign extremists.

Britain is and always will be one of the world's most open and tolerant societies, and it must be careful to draw a line between terrorist-supporting extremist speech and legitimate peaceful political dissent. Britain can no longer tolerate the Islamic militancy in its midst, which seeks to destroy British society and impose an Islamic state. Every effort must be made to energize Muslim leaders in Britain to work actively against the extremists in their communities.

The United States should strongly support Britain's anti-terrorist measures, which are clearly aimed at the "preachers of hate" who played an instrumental role in radicalizing British Muslims. Their enactment will not only increase British security, but American security as well.

## The United Nations Lacks Moral Courage

Predictably, the strongest opposition to elements of the UK's [United Kingdom's] anti-terror plans has come from the United Nations [UN]. The UN's "special rapporteur on torture," Manfred Nowak, has criticized the plan to deport extremists to countries such as Jordan and has called on the

British government to reverse its plan to draw up memorandums of understanding with Middle Eastern and African countries. Nowak is appointed by the discredited UN Commission on Human Rights, whose membership includes brutal dictatorships such as Sudan and Cuba. The Commission, meanwhile, is threatening to report Britain for human rights violations to the UN General Assembly when it meets in September. The UN High Commissioner for Refugees has also condemned Britain's deportation proposals.

Once again, the UN, which has struggled for decades to reach a definition of terrorism and whose failed leadership is reeling from a series of major scandals, demonstrates its lack of moral clarity on the world stage, as well as its arrogant eagerness to intervene in the national security affairs of a sovereign democratic state.

As the Home Secretary remarked in an interview with British television,

> The human rights of those people who were blown up on the Tube in London on July 7 are, to be quite frank, more important than the human rights of the people who committed those acts. . . . I wish the UN would look at human rights in the round rather than simply focusing all the time on the terrorist.

The United Nations must be reminded that appeasement of violent extremists is always doomed to failure. The British government, along with the United States, should strongly reject the hectoring of unelected UN bureaucrats and call for the world body to take a more positive role in combating international terrorism.

## More Anti-Terrorism Laws Are Needed

British Prime Minister Tony Blair has demonstrated outstanding leadership in the seven weeks since the July 7 attacks. He is the most visible public face of the global war against terrorism. While actively engaging moderate Muslim leaders, Blair has clearly identified the threat the West is facing today: the evil ideology advanced by Islamic extremists whose ultimate goals are the destruction of liberal democracy across the world and the establishment of a Muslim caliphate. This is an ideology that cannot be appeased or negotiated with, but must be defeated. [Blair has stated:]

> Its roots are not superficial, but deep, in the madrasses [Islamic schools] of Pakistan, in the extreme forms of Wahabi doctrine in Saudi Arabia, in the former training camps of al-Qaeda in Afghanistan, in the cauldron of Chechnya, in parts of the politics of most countries in the Middle East and many in Asia; in the extremist minority that now in every European city preach hatred of the West and our way of life.

Blair has also stood firm on the British commitment to the people of Iraq and has vowed not to be intimidated into withdrawing British forces from the country. Unlike his Spanish counterpart Prime Minister Jose Luis Rodriguez Zapatero, Blair will not allow the foreign policy of his country to be dictated by barbaric terrorists.

---

*The London bombings also highlighted the need for greater powers of detention of terrorist suspects.*

---

## Great Britain Must Protect Its Citizens First

Still, the Blair administration can and must do more to combat the terrorist threat. Britain cannot fight this war with one hand tied behind its back, constrained by European conventions that weigh more heavily in favor of the rights of the terrorist than those of the British public. The incorporation into British law of the European Convention on Human Rights (ECHR) was a major error of judgment that fundamentally undermined both national sovereignty and the ability of Her

Majesty's government to protect her own citizens. The Human Rights Act of 1998 must be amended if the new anti-terror laws are to be fully implemented, and the UK should immediately withdraw from any provision of the ECHR that weakens British national security. Further, Parliament should debate a withdrawal from the Convention as a whole.

The London bombings also highlighted the need for greater powers of detention of terrorist suspects. The UK should enact legislation that permits the indefinite preventive detention of suspected terrorists in secure prison facilities. House arrest provisions and "control orders" such as curfews and tagging are not powerful enough to deter terrorists. In order to ensure a fair system of checks and balances, individual suspects' cases should be subject to periodic review by British (not European) courts.

## Britain Should Adopt a Version of the USA PATRIOT Act

The British government should consider several measures pioneered in the highly successful USA PATRIOT Act, including increased surveillance authorities for British police and the prevention of charities from providing assistance to terrorist organizations. U.S. and British authorities should employ a far greater degree of coordination in counterterrorist measures, and the Blair government should show a greater willingness to extradite terrorism suspects wanted for trial in the United States. As well, Washington and London should carefully coordinate their lists of terrorist groups.

---

*For far too long, Islamic radicals preached sedition and hatred while protected by a naïve policy of "see no evil, hear no evil."*

---

At the same time, both the [George W.] Bush Administration and the U.S. Congress should strongly consider importing aspects of British anti-terror legislation that may be beneficial, especially rules governing the deportation and exclusion of foreign extremists. In addition, the White House should follow the lead set by Downing Street and adopt a more aggressive stance in clearly defining the United States' enemy in the global war on terror.

## United Against Terrorism

Great Britain is at war, and times of great danger and turmoil require extraordinary measures in the interests of national security. The new anti-terror provisions are a major step in the right direction. They will send a clear message that Britain is no longer a safe haven for Islamic militants and terrorist organizations. Other European governments will no doubt seek to emulate this stance with similar measures.

The British bulldog tradition of strength and resilience in the face of adversity has returned with a vengeance. The culture of liberal complacency that dominated the domestic thinking of a large swathe of Britain's political elite since the passing of the Thatcher era is finally coming to an end. For far too long, Islamic radicals preached sedition and hatred while protected by a naïve policy of "see no evil, hear no evil."

The twilight of Britain's age of innocence has coincided with a sharp renewal of the Anglo-U.S. special relationship, which had shown signs of strain in the months before the bombers hit London. Ironically, the terrorists, for whom a central goal was to divide Britain and the United States, have only succeeded in strengthening ties between the two nations. At no time since the Second World War has joint British and American leadership been more important on the world stage. Indeed, the greatest threat to al-Qaeda's twisted vision is the enduring alliance between Washington and London.

# Organizations to Contact

**American Civil Liberties Union (ACLU)**
125 Broad St., 18th Fl., New York, NY    10004
(212) 344-3005 • fax: (212) 344-2218
e-mail: aclu@aclu.org
Web site: www.aclu.org

The ACLU is a national organization that works to defend Americans' civil rights guaranteed in the U.S. Constitution. The ACLU publishes Action Alerts on a variety of issues; some alerts related to hate speech include "Free Speech," "Privacy and Technology," and "Racial Justice."

**Anti-Defamation League (ADL)**
823 United Nations Plaza, New York, NY    10017
(212) 885-7700
e-mail: www.adl.org
Web site: www.adl.org

The ADL is an international organization that fights prejudice and extremism. It collects, organizes, and distributes information about anti-Semitism, hate crimes, bigotry, and racism, and also monitors hate groups and extremists on the Internet. Among its many publications are *How to Combat Hate Crimes: An ADL Blueprint for Action* and *Hate Crimes: An ADL Approach*. Its online resources include *The Quiet Retooling of the Militia Movement, Extremism: The High Price of Policing Hate,* and *Jihad: Islamic Terrorists and the Internet*.

**Council of American-Islamic Relations (CAIR)**
453 New Jersey Ave. SE, Washington, DC    20003-4034
(202) 488-8787 • fax: (202) 488-0833
e-mail: cair@cair-net.org
Web site: www.cair-net.org

CAIR's mission is to enhance understanding of Islam, encourage dialogue, protect civil liberties, empower American Muslims, and build coalitions that promote justice and mutual understanding. Established in 1994, the council works to promote a positive image of Islam and Muslims in America. CAIR issues Action Alerts on civil rights, political activism, challenging hate, and understanding Islam.

**Eagle Forum**
PO Box 618, Alton, IL   62002
(618) 462-5415 • fax: (618) 462-8909
e-mail: eagle@eagleforum.org
Web site: www.eagleforum.org

The Eagle Forum is a national grassroots organization of eighty thousand conservative men and women who share pro-family values. Owned by Phyllis Schlafly, the forum publishes numerous alerts on feminism, politics, education, national defense, and constitutional issues. The forum is best known for the monthly *Phyllis Schlafly Report*, which has been published since 1967, and the *Education Reporter*.

**Federal Bureau of Investigations (FBI)**
935 Pennsylvania Ave. NW, Washington, DC   20535-0001
(202) 324-3000
Web site: www.fbi.gov/

The FBI's Uniform Crime Reporting Program began in 1929 in order to meet a need for reliable, uniform crime statistics for the nation. The bureau's uniform crime statistics are produced from data provided by almost seventeen thousand law enforcement agencies across the United States. Its many annual publications include *Crime in the United States, Hate Crime Statistics*, and *Law Enforcement Officers Killed and Assaulted*.

**Foundation for Individual Rights in Education (FIRE)**
601 Walnut St., Suite 510, Philadelphia, PA   19106
(215) 717 3473 • fax: (215) 717-3440

e-mail: fire@thefire.org
Web site: www.thefire.org

FIRE's core mission is to protect the unprotected and to educate the public and communities of concerned Americans about the threats to their freedom of speech, legal equality, right to due process, religious liberty, and sanctity of conscience—the essential qualities of individual liberty and dignity. FIRE publishes a number of reports, including *Guides to Free Speech on Campus, Guides to Due Process and Fair Procedure on Campus*, and *Guide to Religious Liberty on Campus*.

**Human Rights First (HRF)**
333 Seventh Ave., 13th Fl., New York, NY   10001-5108
(212) 845 5200 • fax: (212) 845 5299
e-mail: gladstonej@humanrightsfirst.org
Web site: www.humanrightsfirst.org

The HRF, formerly known as Lawyers Committee for Human Rights, has worked in the United States and abroad to create a secure and humane world—advancing justice, human dignity, and respect for the rule of law. All its activities are financed by private contributions. It has helped lead the effort to build the capacity of national legal systems to deal with discrimination, hate crimes, and human rights abuses. The organization publishes *Everyday Fears: Hate Crimes in a Time of Intolerance* and *Anti-Semitism in Europe: Challenging Official Indifference*.

**National Association for the Advancement
of Colored People (NAACP)**
4805 Mt. Hope Dr., Baltimore, MD   21215-3297
(877) NAACP-98 • fax: (410) 486-6683
e-mail: youth@naacpnet.org
Web site:: www.naacp.org

The NAACP is the oldest and largest civil rights organization in the United States. Its principal objective is to ensure the political, educational, social, and economic equality of minorities. It publishes the magazine *Crisis* ten times a year as well as a variety of newsletters, books, and pamphlets.

## National Coalition of Anti-Violence Programs (NCAVP)
240 W. Thirty-fifth St., Suite 200, New York, NY  10001
(212) 714-1184 • fax: (212) 714-2627
e-mail: info@ncavp.org
Web site: www.ncavp.org

The NCAVP is a coalition of programs that document and advocate for victims of anti-LGBT and anti-HIV/AIDS violence/harassment, domestic violence, sexual assault, police misconduct, and other forms of victimization. The NCAVP supports existing antiviolence organizations and emerging local programs in their efforts to document and prevent such violence. The organization publishes an annual report on national hate crimes, national domestic violence, and anti-LGBT violence.

## National Coalition of the Homeless (NCH)
2201 P St. NW, Washington, DC  20037
(202) 462-4822 • fax: (202) 462-4823
e-mail: info@nationalhomeless.org
Web site: www.nationalhomeless.org

The NCH engages in public education, policy advocacy, and grassroots organizing. It focuses on housing justice, economic justice, health-care justice, and civil rights. The coalition launched the Bringing America Home Campaign to end homelessness. Two of its most recent fact sheets are "Hate Crimes and Violence Against People Experiencing Homelessness" and "Why Are People Homeless?"

## National Gay and Lesbian Task Force (NGLTF)
2320 Seventeenth St. NW, Washington, DC  20009-2702
(202) 332-6483 • fax: (202) 332-0207
e-mail: ngltf@ngltf.org
Web site: www.ngltf.org

The NGLTF is a civil rights organization that fights bigotry and violence against gays and lesbians. It sponsors conferences and organizes local groups to promote civil rights legislation for gays and lesbians. It publishes the monthly *Eye on Equality* column and distributes reports, fact sheets, and bibliographies on antigay violence.

## National Organization for Women (NOW)
1100 H St. NW, 3rd Fl., Washington, DC   20005
(202) 628-8669 (628-8NOW) • fax: (202) 785-8576
Web site: www.now.org

NOW works to eliminate discrimination and harassment in the workplace, schools, the justice system, and all other sectors of society; to secure abortion, birth control, and reproductive rights for all women; to end all forms of violence against women; to eradicate racism, sexism, and homophobia; and to promote equality and justice in our society. NOW publishes reports on abortion rights, same-sex marriage, and affirmative action. It issues its e-newsletter *National NOW Times* three times a year.

## Organization for the Security and Co-operation of Europe (OSCE)
Kaerntner Ring 5-7, Vienna   1010
   Austria
+43-1 514 36 0 • fax: +43-1 514 36 96
e-mail: info@osce.org
Web site: www.osce.org

The OSCE actively supports its fifty-five member countries in combating all forms of racism, xenophobia, anti-Semitism, and discrimination. It cooperates and coordinates its activities in this field with other European and United Nations organizations such as the European Commission Against Racism and Intolerance, the European Monitoring Centre on Racism and Xenophobia, and the United Nations Committee on the Elimination of Racial Discrimination. The OSCE publishes the monthly *OSCE Magazine*, which promotes tolerance, nondiscrimination, and minority rights.

## Southern Poverty Law Center (SPLC)
400 Washington Ave., Montgomery, AL   36104
(334) 956-8200
Web site: www.splcenter.org

The center litigates civil cases to protect the rights of poor people, particularly when those rights are threatened by hate and extremist groups. The center publishes the monthly *Intelligence Report*, which monitors hate groups and extremist activities, and *Hatewatch*, a frequent e-newsletter, compiling hate news stories across the country. Almost sixty thousand law enforcement officers nationwide turn to the center for information on hate and extremist groups.

# Bibliography

## Books

Donald Altschiller    *Hate Crimes: A Reference Handbook.* Santa Barbara, CA: ABC-CLIO, 2005.

Jeannine Bell    *Policing Hatred: Law Enforcement, Civil Rights, and Hate Crime.* New York: New York University Press, 2002.

Kathleen M. Blee    *Inside Organized Racism: Women in the Hate Movement.* Berkeley and Los Angeles: University of California Press, 2002.

Donald Alexander Downs    *Restoring Free Speech and Liberty on Campus.* Oakland, CA: Independent Institute, 2005.

William Dudley, ed.    *Freedom of Speech.* San Diego: Greenhaven, 2005.

Aladdin Elaasar    *Silent Victims: The Plight of Arab and Muslim Americans in Post 9/11 America.* Bloomington, IN: AuthorHouse, 2004.

Abby L. Ferber    *Home-Grown Hate: Gender and Organized Racism.* New York: Routledge, 2004.

Colin Flint    *Spaces of Hate: Geographies of Discrimination and Intolerance in the U.S.A.* New York: Routledge, 2004.

| Marvin D. Free | *Racial Issues in Criminal Justice: The Case of African Americans.* Westport, CT: Praeger, 2003. |

Katharine Gelber — *Speaking Back: The Free Speech Versus Hate Speech Debate.* Philadelphia: John Benjamins, 2002.

Phyllis B. Gerstenfeld — *Hate Crimes: Causes, Controls, and Controversies.* Thousand Oaks, CA: Sage, 2004.

Phyllis B. Gerstenfeld and Diana R. Grant, eds. — *Crimes of Hate: Selected Readings.* Thousand Oaks, CA: Sage, 2004.

Darnell F. Hawkins — *Crime Control and Social Justice: The Delicate Balance.* Westport, CT: Greenwood, 2003.

Michael Henderson — *Forgiveness: Breaking the Chain of Hate.* Newberg, OR: BookPartners, 2002.

Paul Iganski — *The Hate Debate: Should Hate Be Punished as a Crime?* London: Institute for Jewish Policy Research, 2002.

Mary S. Jackson — *Policing in a Diverse Society: Another American Dilemma.* Durham, NC: Carolina Academic Press, 2006.

Valerie Jenness and Ryken Grattet — *Making Hate a Crime: From Social Movement to Law Enforcement.* New York: Russell Sage Foundation, 2004.

Sandra E.
Johnson

*Standing on Holy Ground: A Triumph over Hate Crime in the Deep South.* New York: St. Martin's, 2002.

Janis L. Judson

*Law, Media, and Culture: The Landscape of Hate.* New York: Peter Lang, 2002.

Joyce King

*Hate Crime: The Story of a Dragging in Jasper, Texas.* New York: Pantheon, 2002.

Helmut Kury

*Crime Prevention: New Approaches.* Mainz, Germany: Weisser Ring, 2003.

Jack Levin and
Jack McDevitt

*Hate Crimes Revisited: America's War Against Those Who Are Different.* Boulder, CO: Westview, 2002.

Jack McDevitt

*Bridging the Information Disconnect in National Bias Crime Reporting: Final Report.* Boston: Northeastern University Institute on Race and Justice, 2003.

MariJo Moore

*Genocide of the Mind: New Native American Writing.* New York: Thunder's Mouth, 2003.

Cindy Mur, ed.

*Does the Internet Benefit Society?* Detroit: Greenhaven, 2005.

Marie D. Natoli

*Taking Sides: Clashing Views in Public Policy, Justice, and the Law.* Dubuque, IA: McGraw-Hill, 2006.

David A. Neiwert  *Death on the Fourth of July: The Story of a Killing, a Trial, and Hate Crime in America.* New York: Palgrave Macmillan, 2004.

Barbara Perry, ed.  *Hate and Bias Crime: A Reader.* New York: Routledge, 2003.

Michael R. Ronczkowski  *Terrorism and Organized Hate Crime: Intelligence Gathering, Analysis, and Investigations.* Boca Raton, FL: CRC, 2004.

Stephen Satris  *Taking Sides: Clashing Views on Controversial Moral Issues.* 10th ed. Guilford, CT: McGraw-Hill/Dushkin, 2005.

Alan Sears and Craig Osten  *The Homosexual Agenda: Exposing the Principal Threat to Religious Freedom Today.* Nashville, TN: Broadman & Holman, 2003.

Thomas Streissguth  *Hate Crimes.* New York: Facts On File, 2003.

Carol M. Swain  *The New White Nationalism in America: Its Challenge to Integration.* New York: Cambridge University Press, 2002.

Mamie Till-Mobley  *Death of Innocence: The Story of the Hate Crime That Changed America.* New York: Random House, 2003.

Mary E. Williams, ed.  *Hate Groups.* San Diego: Greenhaven, 2004.

# Periodicals

David M. Adams    "Punishing Hate and Achieving Equality," *Criminal Justice Ethics*, vol. 24, no. 1, Winter/Spring 2005.

Robert J. Boeckmann and Carolyn Turpin-Petrosino    "Understanding the Harm of Hate Crime," *Journal of Social Issues*, vol. 58, no. 2, Summer 2002.

*Christian Science Monitor*    "National Acrimony and a Rise in Hate Crimes," June 3, 2005.

*Christianity Today*    "Evangelism Antagonism: Sharing the Good News Is Not a Hate Crime," vol. 47, no. 2, February 2003.

*Columbus (OH) Dispatch*    "Hate Law Weak and Uneven, Some Say," March 4, 2006.

David Corn    "The Fundamental John Ashcroft," *Mother Jones*, March/April 2002.

*Entertainment Weekly*    "The Matthew Shepard Story," March 8, 2002.

David Goldberger    "The Inherent Unfairness of Hate Crime Statutes," *Harvard Journal of Legislation*, vol. 41, no. 2, Summer 2004.

*Jet*    "Cross-Burning Ban Backed by Supreme Court," April 28, 2003.

Paul Johnson    "'That Man Committed a Hate-Crime.' 'What?' 'Well, He Told a Joke, Didn't He?'" *Spectator*, April 5, 2003.

| | |
|---|---|
| Crystal L. Keels | "The Best-Kept Secret: Crime on Campus," *Black Issues in Higher Education*, vol. 21, no. 6, May 6, 2004. |
| Jane Kramer | "The Patriot: A Militia Leader and His Impatient Followers," *New Yorker*, May 6, 2002. |
| Ian McMillan | "Reducing Crime Against People with Learning Disabilities: Police to Launch National Manual on Dealing with Hate Crimes," *Learning Disability Practice*, vol. 8, no. 1, February 2005. |
| Iain Murray | "Hate Crime Hooey," *American Enterprise*, April/May 2005. |
| *National Catholic Reporter* | "Bishops' Commission Condemns 'Hate Speech,'" January 24, 2003. |
| *Newsweek* | "A Nightmare on the Job." July 21, 2003. |
| Peter Tatchell | "The Reggae Lyrics of Hate," *New Statesman*, September 29, 2003. |
| *Time* | "In Topeka, Hate Mongering Is a Family Affair," February 28, 2005. |
| Eugene Volokh | "Crime-Facilitating Speech," *Stanford Law Review*, vol. 57, no. 4, March 2005. |
| *Washington Monthly* | "The Hate Debate," June 2002. |

*Washington Times*  "Criminalized Thoughts? Hate-Crime Laws Threaten Religious Freedom, Foes Say," December 29, 2004.

*Washington Times*  "Hate-Crime Add-On to Child-Safety Bill Irks House GOP," September 19, 2005.

Christopher Wolf  "Needed: Diagnostic Tools to Gauge the Full Effect of Online Anti-Semitism and Hate," *Journal of Internet Law*, vol. 8, no. 3, September 2004.

## Internet Sources

Stefan M. Beck  "Dartmouth Indians: The New Tradition," *Dartmouth Review*, May 12, 2003. http://www.dartreview.com/archives/2003/05/12/dartmouth_indians_the_new_tradition.php.

*Christianity Today*  "Christian History Corner: Is Speaking Truth a Hate Crime?" August 6, 2004. www.christianitytoday.com/ct/2004/131/53.0.html.

David Horowitz  "Black Racism: The Hate Crime That Dare Not Speak Its Name," *FrontPageMagazine.com*, July 16, 2002. www.frontpagemag.com/Articles/ReadArticle.asp?ID=1912.

Ramesh Ponnuru  "The Case Against Bush Hatred. Hate Crimes" *New Republic*, September 29, 2003. https://ssl.tnr.com/p/docsub.mhtml?i=20030929&s=ponnuru092903

# Index

prejudice
school efforts to combat,
177–78
school violence and, 166, 167
prevention, hate crime
by addressing societal problems, 204
anti-terrorist measures and,
205–10
by individual people, 183–84
organizing alternative event to
hate rally and, 189–90
by political lobbying, 202
pressure on government officials and, 203
by raising money through
hate-group events, 186–88
reasons for, 183–84
ripple effect of, 188–89
for school violence, 174–76
through education, 202–3
by uniting and organizing,
185–86
Princeton Survey Research Associates, 114–15
Project Lemonade, 186–87
*Protocols of the Elders of Zion*, 196
Pryce, Deborah, 62
public opinion
on online hate speech, 114–15
supporting college hate speech
codes, 112–14
Putin, Vladimir, 23

Quebec City (Canada), 27

racism
American Indian mascots,
logos, nicknames and, 117–
19, 122–23
education is an answer to,
123–24
in Europe, 125–26

Racist Skinheads, 13, 163
racist violence
against African students,
22–24
demands enhanced punishment, 70–72
desecration of cemeteries and,
25–27
European football and, 24–25
low-level, 20, 21–22
in Northern Ireland, 21–22
in Russia, 23–24
in schools, 166–68
in Scotland, 20–21
Reno, Janet, 50
reporting, of hate crimes
against the disabled, 81–82
against the homeless, 43–44
law enforcement training and,
48, 49–50
against lesbians, gays, bisexuals and transgendered
people, 31–32
are for minor incidents, 50
against Muslims, 37–38
"Responding to Hate at School"
(Southern Poverty Law Center),
175
restraining orders, 60–62
right-wing hate groups, 14
Roberts, Michael, 42
Romania, 26
Rudenstine, Neil L., 131
Rushville, Missouri, 184–85
Russian Federation, 22–24, 25, 26
Rwanda, 29

SafeClick, 150
SafeSurf, 150
same-sex marriage, 36
Saraceno, Jon, 142, 144
Schlafly, Phyllis, 56
Schlessinger, Laura, 52
Schlotterbeck, Mark, 190